CW00673317

WHAT
WE

LESSONS ON
LIFE, LOVE, LOSS
AND FRIENDSHIP

KNOW
NOW

About the Authors

Jenny and Mairéad's friendship began over twenty years ago when they met working on Today FM's hugely popular *Ray D'Arcy Show*.

Jenny has worked in Irish radio for over 20 years. Before joining *The Ray D'Arcy Show*, she worked on *The Gerry Ryan Show* on 2FM and on East Coast Radio. While with Today FM, she won numerous radio awards with the team. Jenny co-presented the 'Fix-It Friday' slot every week and, with her cupid wings on, she was responsible for getting many listeners together. A career highlight was singing 'Happy Birthday' to Roger Moore. She stepped back from daily radio life in 2017.

Like Jenny, Mairéad has worked in radio for over 20 years, spending 12 of those with *The Ray D'Arcy Show*. Mairéad went on to produce *The Ian Dempsey Breakfast Show* on Today FM, and she has presented *Ireland's Fittest Family* on RTÉ for ten years. She was crowned champion of RTÉ's *Dancing With The Stars* in 2019, after which she returned to Today FM to host *Lunchtime with Mairéad Ronan*. She pressed pause on her radio life in December of 2021 to spend more time with her young family. Mairéad is also co-founder of haircare brand FARO.

Together Jenny and Mairéad present and produce the podcast *Jenny and Mairéad Now*.

WHAT WE KNOW NOW

LESSONS ON LIFE, LOVE, LOSS AND FRIENDSHIP

Jenny Kelly &
Mairéad Ronan

GILL BOOKS

Gill Books

Hume Avenue

Park West

Dublin 12

www.gillbooks.ie

Gill Books is an imprint of M.H. Gill and Co.

9781804581834

Designed by Jane Matthews

Illustrations by Eva Kelly: 151, 160, 178, 194, 208, 215, 220, 223, 232, 248

Illustrations and photos: © Adobe Stock: Gondex, 2; klikline, 224; Line Addict, 239; Olena, 230; Olga Rai, 103; Valenty, 170; Yelyzaveta, 202; © Alamy Stock Photo / Moviestore Collection Ltd, 240; © iStock: Alexander Ryabintsev, 63; ArtUma88, 50; Askhat Giliakhov, 165; Aynur Huseynzade, 84; budi priyanto, 93, 104, 130; Caramel, 120, 138, 152, 188, 213, 216; danang setyo nugroho, 192; Daniil Chaban, 113; Denys Polhun, 13; Dimitris66, 164; juliawhite, 42; LuckyStep48, 89; MegaShabanov, 96; Mironov Konstantin, 31; mitay20, 143; ngupakarti, 95; Olga Furmaniuk, 34; Olga Ubirailo, 46, 54, 96, 119, 261; Tetiana Garkusha, 226, 263; ulimi, 166; Vdant, 196, 198; Volha Kratkouskaya, 189; © Kyran O'Brien, 268.

Copyedited by Kerri Ward

Proofread by Esther Ní Dhonnacha

Printed and bound by Printer Trento, Italy

This book is typeset in Arboria.

The paper used in this book comes from the wood pulp of sustainably managed forests.

A CIP catalogue record for this book is available from the British Library.

5 4 3 2 1

Dedication

For Ray, Kate and Tom, with love

To my BEDLM (Bonnie, Eliza, Dara, Louis and Murphy)

Contents

Introduction

We love a list, so let's start with one.

We have been friends for over 20 years and in that time we have experienced: single life, career highs, break-ups, make-ups, marriages, divorce, pregnancies, miscarriages, babies, diets, hairstyles, fashion, booze endings, work break-ups, endless cleaning, constant what's-for-dinner decisions, stress, holidays, dancing competitions, sadness, sea swimming, death, dogs, arguments and ageing.

Mistakes have been made but solutions have been found.

We are all struggling along trying to make sense of things. There is no handbook to life (even though we secretly believe that some people do have one that they refuse to share with the rest of us) but after A LOT of talking (and cups of tea), we feel that we have hit on one fundamental truth ...

Are you ready?

Life ends and death is final. Ta-da!

So why are we all worrying about stupid shit that, at the end of the day, doesn't really matter?

We are constantly being told that we need to be more Zen and live in the NOW, but let's not forget about the other, more Irish meaning of NOW. Is there any other small word that holds as much meaning for Irish women? That three-letter word said after an inhalation of breath ...

'Now ...' (Tea is finished, what's next on my never-ending to-do list?)

'Now ... ' (That's the end of the discussion, we need to move on.)

'Now ... ' (I've totally forgotten what I was going to do or say next.)

'Now ... ' (I'm sitting down for the first time today and if any person or animal asks me for a thing, I will murder them.)

But even though it's all we have, it's hard to live in the NOW. We need constant signs and reminders. We'd like to have an airplane banner travel the length and breadth of Ireland that read, 'Stop searching. You are enough.' And that is the TRUTH (it deserves caps). But we all need help in realising this. And that's what this book hopes to be — a way to share with you our failures, successes, mess-ups and middle-aged learned lessons. All together maybe we can learn to not take it all so seriously — and that each moment is another lesson to add into your very own handbook of life.

We like to think of this book as a dipper-inner: pick it up, have a flick through and hopefully you will land on something that just might help (or that will at least make you smile) as you navigate the unavoidable ups and downs of your one precious life.

Let's get stuck straight in.

05/21/2005 23:40

What we know now about →

friendship

OR, WHY A GOOD FRIENDSHIP SHOULD FEEL LIKE MARRIAGE, BUT WITHOUT THE SEX

I'm a good friend most of the time ... until I'm not

M I *think* I'm a good friend – I definitely try to be – but like most humans I've gotten things wrong over the years. Those things have damaged some very special and important friendships, including Jenny's and mine.

Life is all about timing and once upon a time our life clocks were not in sync. Neither of us could support the other through our separate trips to Shitsville. It was April 2011, and Jenny's lovely dad Mick had died suddenly. At the time I was desperately trying to find a place to rent that I could afford, I was knee–deep in solicitors' letters with my divorce, trying to unravel my previous life while also trying to jump–start a new one. I genuinely felt that I had nothing to give. We didn't fall out, but we both went quiet and that broke my heart again (it had already taken a big hit). I presumed Jenny didn't want to talk about her dad so I left her to deal with the loss alone. And the result was that both of us ended up broken–hearted.

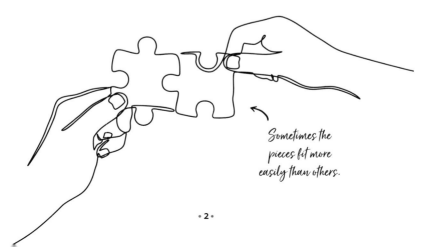

Sometimes the pieces fit more easily than others.

'Have you ever fallen out?'

J **After my dad's sudden death, I wanted to be on my own, but I also wanted Mairéad there with me. I thought that Mairéad would somehow be able to read my mind and know that I needed her to help me get through it all. What about that for unrealistic pressure?**

For the first time since we met, we were distant and couldn't communicate our needs to each other. We were both hurt and confused about what was happening and instead of dealing with it by talking about what was going on, we pulled further and further away from each other.

I thought about her all the time and yet felt like I could do nothing to solve our distance. I pretended outwardly that I WAS FINE. I was not fine.

For me to explain to Mairéad how I was feeling meant being completely vulnerable and opening up, and I wasn't able to do that. So instead, I did nothing. We were polite yet distant when we saw each other, and we missed out on a lot of important moments together. This still makes me sad to this day. There was an obvious simple solution — meet up, talk and get over it. But it didn't seem that simple.

We were both hurt and didn't know where to start. But we did start, slowly. Like two people tip-toeing around each other, we began to talk and open up. Then one day we went on a hike together in Dunmore East, County Waterford.

We had been building up to this moment and being outdoors, walking in nature, allowed us both to fully relax and be honest about what had happened. We finally let our guards down and let it all out. It was such a relief — both of us crying and vowing never, ever again to allow anything come between us.

Real friendship love

I'm not good with dates but I am good at remembering a feeling, and I honestly do remember the moment Mairéad came into my life. It was March 2002 and I was part of a team of three in the Today FM office working on a very busy daily radio show. We were told that there was a girl coming in on work experience who would be helping us out for two weeks. In walked Mairéad with a Ready Brek glow of positivity surrounding her. She slotted right in, like the missing piece of a jigsaw puzzle. It was that easy. From the moment we began talking we did not stop. We laughed a lot, we gossiped, we ate lunch, we went out in the evening for drinks, and did I mention laughing non-stop? It was that instant. A real friendship love, the kind that doesn't come around too often, but when it does you need to grab it with both hands.

05/18/2005 19:06

That Ready Brek glow of positivity

How Jenny and I met

M I'm from Finglas, Jenny is from Foxrock. The only thing they have in common is that they are both in Dublin and begin with F. When we first met in the old offices of Today FM, I was 21 and Jenny was 29 — not exactly the basis of a budding best friendship. But Jenny welcomed me to the team with her big dirty laugh and loud, sexy voice, and very quickly she became such an important person in my life.

We worked hard together and partied even harder. We have roared laughing — the kind of laughing where you can't breathe — and we've bawled our eyes out together, too. She supported me greatly during some of the worst times in my life by just being there, even including me on her family holidays. In the summer of 2008, we said goodbye in the office on a Friday and met up in the airport on Saturday morning to go to Portugal for two weeks. Herself with Ray and their little girl Kate, and me with my son Dara, who was two years old at the time. The following year, Dara and I were included in Jenny and Ray's bank holiday plans in West Cork and again on their two-week summer holiday to Spain. In total, we spent over 12 years working side by side, until Jenny needed to step back from work (more on that later!).

I can say whole-heartedly that I completely trust Jenny and I know that she trusts me. I love being in her company and even if I was in it all day yesterday, today is a new day and there are still so many chats to have. Being with Jenny is easy — like a kids' jigsaw puzzle, we just fit. It's always calming, it's always a laugh and I will always and forever love her dearly. We were meant to be friends and I feel so lucky that we are.

A good friendship is basically a marriage – but without the sex

Or at least that's what it should be. So what are the signs of a great friendship?

- You look forward to spending time with them.
- You want to help when they are in need.
- You feel better for being in their company.
- You don't always agree with one another, but will stand by their decisions (and they will stand by yours).
- They fill your cup.
- They let you rant.
- There is always laughter.
- They tell you the truth – sometimes what you don't want to hear.
- They celebrate your wins and comfort you on your losses ... and you do exactly the same for them.

I'm careful with how I use the word 'friend'. I don't throw it around like popcorn at a kids' party. I keep it as a special title for those in my life who I've really let in. I have 15 of them, which sounds like a small number for someone who has lived for 44 years. But because they are all either individuals or in small groups, it means I can maintain these friendships in a real way. Plus, I *want* to, because these people are really important to me. Some of them are men (shocker!), some I've known since I was a child, others I met after I turned 30. But with all of them there is trust, honesty and support in abundance, and the best thing is that I never feel like I have to filter myself around them.

Sisters are bonus besties

I'm very lucky to have two much older* sisters, who most of the time double up as best friends (we have also wanted to kill one another many times #normal). As a kid I could never have seen this happening – the age gap was too wide. I always loved them, but the only things we had in common at the time were Mam, Dad, our home address and a love of George Michael (they introduced me to George). But around the age of 17, as if by magic, my sisters became more than my sisters – they became my friends. The age gap seemed to close overnight. We still liked the same music but now that I'd stopped wearing Man United jerseys we could share clothes, too. I also ditched my Chicago Bulls hoodie in favour of dresses from Oasis, Warehouse, Morgan and Mango. At 18 I even began to join them on nights out in town! We were like the Corrs but without brother Jim. It was also the first time I experienced brutal honesty – the kind that only comes from a good place: 'Mairéad, you need to stop wearing blue eyeshadow.' None of my teenage friends had the heart to tell me this. Over the years, my gorgeous sisters gave me the thumbs-up on some relationships and the thumbs-down on others, they comforted me, supported me, championed me and they both did their best to mother me after our mam died. But no matter what, we have always been the best of friends – because just sharing DNA wasn't enough. Sometimes life has a way of pulling you towards the place you're meant to be, whether that's a friend, a partner or even a job.

*Simone is twelve years older than me and Olga is nine years older than me. The 'much older' thing is a long-standing family joke that will stay until my last breath … sorry, girls. Ⓜ

True friends allow you to be exactly who you are

J **Confession: Sometimes I am not a good friend.**

- I don't like talking on the phone.

- I'm terrible at remembering dates.

- I don't really like going out after 6 p.m.

- If I do manage to see you it might be weeks till you hear from me again.

Wow – what a catch!

Some of you are probably reading this and thinking, 'How the hell does she have any friends?', but I know there are others thinking, 'She's my kinda gal!' I think the reason my friends put up with me is because we have known each other so long and have seen each other in so many different phases of life that we are accepting (mostly) of these personality idiosyncrasies.

What I know about friendships

As a woman in my 50s, here's what I've learned about friendships and what makes them last.

Friendships should be fluid and easy – not based on obligation and tension. You are two people who choose to be together when you can because you love each other. It's as simple as that. To make a new friend now, at my age, I have to have that feeling – you know the one, where you just think, 'Yes! I love her! She's in.' That's only happened to me a few times in the last 20 years, so the odds of my friend circle growing are not great. But is that so bad? Have we all bought into the idea of what we've been told it means to be a good female friend? We put a huge amount of pressure on ourselves to live up to this ideal standard – and I wonder if this is why so many women feel so overwhelmed a lot of the time. Along with all the effort they have to put into their work relationships, their home life and their immediate family, they also have to juggle mum friends, old school friends and college friends. It's just too much.

Friendships ebb and flow – and that's OK Controversial statement here, but I don't think you should have to maintain a friendship. It sounds like too much hard work. There will be ebb and flow in the relationship, but the minute pressure is put on a friendship, things will start to go wrong. It's like the needy wannabe boyfriend or girlfriend chasing after you – what does that make you want to do? RUN THE OTHER WAY. I'm not suggesting that you make absolutely no effort with a friend and then expect everything to be rosy when you next meet up. What I mean is that true friendship is based on security and the knowledge that even when you are apart or things are a little distant, the relationship remains.

It's easy in the modern world for jealousies to arise. Say you haven't met up with a friend in ages, but every time you see her on Instagram she seems to be out having a ball at a different do or event. As we all know, the reality can be very different to what is presented online. I know that I've been at events that I didn't want to be at – got dolled up and smiled for the pictures – but I was actually dreaming about being at home in my Birkenstocks and cosy dressing gown. To a friend feeling left out, all they see is the bright smile and the night out – without them.

When you are feeling let down by a friend, ask yourself what you get from the relationship Sometimes a walk and a chat will clear the air, but other times you have to recognise that maybe you expect and need different things from the friendship. But before you go in all guns blazing looking to ditch this friend, maybe stop and think about what you DO get from the friendship. Looking to her to be everything to you is never going to work, and that's why it's good to have multiple friends who fulfil different needs within you. Acceptance of who your friend is will change the dynamic immediately. You will stop looking to her to fulfil every single one of your friendship needs and just enjoy her for what she can and does give in the relationship. It all goes back to when I was talking about change earlier – ebb and flow – allowing people to be themselves and accepting that.

We have to know when to say goodbye to a relationship and we have to know that it's OK to do that, too It's very un-Irish to have a break-up conversation with a friend – most of us would probably find it easier to just ghost that person. I was ghosted once by an old friend. We reconnected by chance and then when we tried to meet up a few times, life got in the way. When I eventually tried to arrange a meeting she had blocked me on all socials. And I was fine with it.

Breaking up with a friend means confronting the situation and telling the person the 'why'. If it's too hard to do this face to face there are other options. You could go old-school and write a letter – this is a good way to get your thoughts in order and also keeps you from getting into a tit-for-tat row. You could text the person and say that you need to talk to them about something important and ask if they can take a call. This will set them up to expect something and hopefully means they won't be caught off guard. But probably the best thing to do is meet for a coffee and just say what's on your mind. It's going to be awkward, but when it's done, it's done. Like I said, this is the hardest option but probably the most respectful and honest.

REAL
FRIENDSHIP
DOESN'T COME
AROUND TOO
OFTEN, BUT
WHEN IT DOES
YOU NEED TO
GRAB IT
WITH BOTH
HANDS.

Frenemies

A frenemy is a friend who's also a little bit of an enemy — if you can be a 'little bit' of an enemy. It's a person you're friendly with, but there is a bit of dislike there, too. A rivalry, a distrust, a feeling of things being not quite right ... as Britney said, it's all a bit toxic.

It might be a once-over of your outfit when you meet up, a dig at your weight, a humorous put-down in front of others that somehow feels a lot like being shamed. But you don't say or do anything because, sure, it's just them and they've always been like that ... but maybe pause there for a bit and have a think about that. Is it OK for a so-called friend to talk to you, or about you, that way? Is it right that you feel 'less than' around them? Is it OK that you dread seeing their name come up when your mobile rings? The answer is pretty simple: No!

The way I see it is, if you allow someone to treat you or speak to you that way then you have to accept being treated and spoken to that way. My advice would be to take a deep breath and gently confront the situation by saying something like, 'I'd prefer it if you didn't mention my weight', or, 'That sounded a bit mean — is there something that you want to talk to me about?'

My advice is to say, 'Was that comment meant to be helpful or hurtful?' It will stop them in their tracks! Ⓜ

You will cause the person to stop and think a little, and if they continue to speak to you and treat you the same way you now know that it is intentional. The next move is yours. Do you continue to allow yourself to be treated this way? Do you feel you are not worth kindness and love? Do you think that people's words don't mean anything? And before I go on, I'll answer all the above with a big shouty NO (in caps).

Usually when we try to explain away someone's behaviour it's because we are too scared to confront the truth because it means that we will have to take action. Life is too bloody short to allow toxic people in your space. If you are not feeling brave, then speak to a good friend about the situation and ask them to back you up when you are next in this person's company — they can give you strength. If you start standing up for yourself, slowly but surely you will begin to feel more confident and you'll be able to start shaking off frenemies like this one.

Aim for quality over quantity

The 'Dunbar's number' study was published in the 1990s by evolutionary psychologist Robin Dunbar. He claimed that humans can cognitively handle up to 150 meaningful social relationships (150!!!). But out of all these connections, the number of close friendships people have, Dunbar found, is five. That sounds a bit more reasonable to me. That group of five friends should be your inner sanctum, the friends who you know and trust implicitly and vice versa. These are the people that you are totally yourself with — no need for any pretence or for putting a face on. They get you and you get them. They are a joy to be around because there is no effort required. It feels easy and relaxed and even on the off days when you are not feeling it, you can be truthful and tell them. These five people (and for some people this number could be two or three) might not be a group but could be individuals from different times in your life that, for whatever reason, you clicked with.

The magic number

A real friendship bond

There is a loneliness epidemic in Ireland. Out of the whole of Europe, we came top of the table in a loneliness study that was published in 2023. This makes me feel so sad. A stark finding in the study was that, although being in a relationship is associated with lower loneliness, those in unhappy relationships are more likely to be lonely than single people. To have people around you but still be feeling lonely is a dark place to be.

The good news is that having several close friendships is linked to a lower risk of loneliness. That seems pretty obvious, yet for so many people that feeling of loneliness still persists. And this is where authenticity comes into play.

You can have lots of friends, but if you do not allow yourself to be vulnerable with some of them and to be your real, true self, then you will feel misunderstood, removed and ... well ... lonely. I say this as someone who finds it difficult to show vulnerability. I was raised and praised to be strong and resilient. It's hard to let those barriers down and to admit when things are difficult or my feelings are bruised, but what I have found as I get older is that the more I do this with trusted friends, the lighter and happier I feel. It is true that a weight is lifted when a problem is shared. A gentle admission of how you are really feeling allows a space to open up between you and a friend that creates closeness and a real friendship bond.

As we get older our friend circle may become smaller but it also becomes stronger. The people we call our friends are so important in our lives, but we can all get things wrong. Life is complicated. Things happen. We both know this only too well. But what we know now is that when friendships break down, there is a way back. It takes time and patience and a lot of love. But it's worth it. That's what friends are for.

TRUE FRIENDSHIP IS A BALM FOR LONELINESS.

09/23/2004 07:10

What we know now about

relationships

OR, WHY THE FIRST CUT IS THE DEEPEST

Blind dates

M When we first began the podcast, we immediately started getting emails from listeners asking us when we were going to put on singles' nights, like we used to do on our radio show.

We had started by doing the first speed dating events in Ireland. If you're not familiar with them, this involves you sitting in front of someone for about five minutes and having a quick chat, and then a bell rings and you move on to the next date. If you liked the person, you ticked a box, and if they ticked yours too, we exchanged email addresses on your behalf. We also did lots of 'Blind Date' on the radio, with Ray D'Arcy as Cilla – this was great fun. All the daters had to go on were the answers to questions Ray asked.

Then there was another tour of the country with 'Strictly Come Dating', which involved dancing with everyone in the room ... The night began with a dance lesson from Brian Redmond of *Dancing with the Stars* fame. But we realised on all of the singles' nights that the women were glammed up and the men were, well, not. So we decided to force the men into dressing up a bit and making more of an effort by taking a bunch of singles to mingle at the Punchestown races. It was without a doubt our wildest singles' event (and it may have been our last). A lot of these have resulted in marriages and babies because we have always been very good at getting people together – hence our nicknames back then: Cupid Kelly and Cupid Farrell.

Although at this stage of our lives we both feel that we've hit our stride when it comes to love, our relationship histories are far from perfect and there have been lots of ups and downs for both of us along the way.

My first REAL crush (on someone who wasn't a member of Take That or a Dublin footballer!) was 'him'. I was 12 years old, he was 14. I was small, he was tall. I had braces, his adult teeth had arrived down perfectly straight. I was plain and he was extremely gorgeous in the face department. I was single (of course I was, I had just made my Confirmation) but he had a girlfriend, and she was the most beautiful girl in our estate in Finglas.

I spent years just looking out for him ... or looking at him from afar whenever I had the chance. Of course, I would turn a bright shade of scarlet whenever he said hello, which he did a lot because he had impeccable manners too. There is an entry in my *Beverly Hills, 90210*-themed diary from 1993 where the entire day was summed up with, 'Saw him today, he said hello to me by moving his eyebrows up and nodding his head.' Whatever else happened that day didn't matter because this was the BIG event and needed to be written down and remembered for ever.

Teenage crushes are commonly perceived as cute, innocent fun, but when those feelings aren't reciprocated, it can trigger a range of negative thoughts and emotions (hang on while I roll up my trousers — I'm going in deep here!). My crush on him was one-sided, and over time it meant that I saw myself as not being good enough for someone that I really liked, and that created a sense of self-doubt. For years I believed that someone like him would never even notice someone as ordinary as me and that I was in some way invisible.

Throughout my formative years this internal chatter continued. I have to note that he wasn't to blame, nor were my parents, who did nothing only tell me how wonderful I was. It took me years (yes, years!) to recover from that crush. It wasn't merely getting over him as an individual but also unlearning the lessons I believed my crush on him had taught me.

He's just not that into you

By the time I hit my 20s I had finally embraced the lesson I had *actually* learned — that sometimes you really like someone, and they don't like you back, and that's shit but it's OK. It's not a reflection of your worth and there are plenty of other people out there who will appreciate how bloody brilliant you are.

But then there are the next-level crushes — the ones where they do more than say hello with their eyebrows. They ask for your number, they ask you out on a date but then act very cool in the days after. Then they text again, there's another date, they go cold again... I have been in this exact situation and I allowed this to continue because I was crushing HARD on this fella. But I knew that for me he was a 'definitely' and for him I was just a 'maybe', and I never wanted to be anyone's maybe. So I finally said goodbye and let go of that crush.

Ultimately the chances of you really liking someone and them liking you back to the same degree and at the same time involves a whole lotta luck. So if you can, stick to the celeb crushes because they won't hurt your feelings or sow any seeds of self-doubt (although I know deep down that Roger Federer would have fallen head over heels in love with me, but alas we just never had the chance to meet... yet!).

Sweet dreams are made of this

SOMETIMES YOU REALLY LIKE SOMEONE, AND THEY DON'T LIKE YOU BACK, AND THAT'S SHIT BUT IT'S OK.

It's just a little crush

J Michael J. Fox FOR EVER — that's what I wrote over and over again in my school copybook. His poster hung above my bed and I kissed him goodnight every night. That floppy brown hair, cheeky yet lovable grin — he was adorable. I couldn't tell you how many times I've watched all the *Back to The Future* movies — and the fact that his character's girlfriend was called Jennifer, well, *swoon*! But at least I had the good grace to have a crush on a movie star and not a real person. Now that would have been very embarrassing!

Except I did. It was 1986, I was in second year and he was in sixth year — to save his modesty, I'll call him 'D'. He was gorgeous. I wasn't the only one to think so — there were quite a few D fans around the school — but I think I may have taken it to a new level when it came to mortifying moments. You see, back then, a million years ago when I was 14, we didn't have digital cameras or camera phones, so I had gone out of my way to pick up an actual disposable camera and was ready to pounce the moment he appeared. I made sure to have my badly cut fringe brushed down and my favourite purple top on and I waited ... and waited ... until finally he walked by and I casually said, 'Hi D, can I get a photo taken with you?' OH YES, I DID. To be fair to him, he stopped and put his arm around me as if he'd been doing this every day for all his life, and SNAP, the picture was taken. I stuck that on my bedroom wall too! In fact, I still have that photo.

FYI, that's Jenny's smug smile.

M

One day on the radio I was asked who I fancied from afar, and I naively answered, 'My crushes? Oh, I like Michael Palin and Rick Stein,' obviously not realising that this was going to be used against me for a very long time. 'OLD GUYS,' everyone shouts, 'Jesus Christ – Daddy issues!'

But I meant crush in a non-sexual way – in an 'I want to sit around chatting with them and looking into their kind eyes' kind of way. OK, that sounds even worse, but that was my dream. And to my absolute horror, one day my dream/nightmare came true. It was my birthday, we were in the studio as usual and Mairéad was putting a caller up on air to speak to Ray. I was looking through some listener texts, not really paying attention, when the red on-air light comes on and I hear Ray saying, 'Good morning, Rick – Jenny, put on your headphones there.' And to my absolute mortification, there on the line was Rick Stein wishing me a happy birthday.

So have a crush, a little fantasy dream – I think it's healthy and fun and gives you a little pep in your step. Just maybe don't hang pictures of them up on your bedroom wall like you did when you were 12.

The Spark

I have set up quite a few of my friends over the years, and yet the irony is that I was not exactly the best when it came to my own relationships.

I had male friends in my teens and a few crushes, but no boyfriends. I was far too immature and really didn't have a clue what it meant to be in a relationship. In college when we all started going 'out out', what usually happened was a gang of us would spend hours getting ready, go out to the pub, get pissed, go to a club and hopefully get a snog.

I was 23 years old before I had my first official, long-term boyfriend. We were together for five years and lived together for the last year. He was the loveliest person, but we were not meant to be (and on that point, I think there should be whole books written about splitting

We were brought together by work, so it was messy and complicated.

up with someone and the pain of missing their family as well as the person. It's so hard for everyone involved).

When Ray started working in Today FM in August 2000, I was told that I would be working as part of his team. I had just split up from that long-term relationship and I spent those first few weeks before we went on air in September crying in the office. Ray thought he had inherited a lunatic on his new radio team (this is an ongoing joke between us: that he did not choose to have me on the team but inherited me instead). Very slowly we became work friends. Creating a new radio show was a very intense and exciting time. We are both stubborn and wanted things done our own way, which caused many heated discussions. Work took over my whole life. We spent nearly all of our time together in Today FM and travelling to and from outside broadcasts all over the country. And after some years (yes, years) a spark began to ignite. We were brought together by work, so it was messy and complicated. It's a wonder for me to look back on now, as it seems like a lifetime ago and, honestly, there was so much drama. The mad thing is that we are not the dramatic type of couple at all now. The biggest row we'll get into these days is over the most mundane nonsense, like not picking up a wet towel or forgetting to put the bin out. I do think that some relationships are like that in the beginning — it's like you are getting all the crap out of the way so that the actual, real relationship can begin. One thing I was certain of, pretty much from the beginning, was that we were meant to be together. I don't know why I was so sure, but I was. I fell deeply in love with him. And as I always tell him, he is SO lucky that he got me in the end.

Singles' events

It was always a struggle to get the men to come along to our singles' events. The emails we got from female listeners who were looking for a partner all say pretty much the same thing: how difficult it is to meet someone these days. But all of them seemed fantastic and so willing to put themselves out there in order to find love.

So, why are all these amazing single people out here, and why can't they find their Mr or Mrs Right? Is it just a case of going on date after date after date until you finally (hopefully) click with someone? Or do you throw your hands up and just get on with living your life with an attitude of 'What will be will be'? That would be fine if it weren't for biological clocks. And I think that is the nub of it; men are just not thinking the same way as women are. They technically have all the time in the world, whereas we don't. (This is of course assuming you want children. Feel free to skip over this bit if you have made that decision to be child free.) Women who want children have to be focused and truthful in their search for a partner. I'm not suggesting you bring up a PowerPoint of all your favourite baby names on the first date, but I am saying that you have to keep your time in mind. Do not entertain time–wasters.

Of course, there are lots of ways to love. Some of us come to realise that the friendships in our lives are our deepest loves, or our nieces and nephews or our animals. Life surprises you when you least expect it and all you can do is live your life for you and not be waiting for that extra something or someone to make you complete.

But in saying all that, sometimes we need a kick up the arse to get back out there and start looking, and the fact is that we are particularly good at setting people up. It's one of our superpowers (along with sleeping). So if you have a single brother or sister or best friend, then send them our way – we're compiling a file. In the meantime, if you're looking for love yourself, here are some thoughts on how to find it.

The snog or the shift

A long, long time ago, there was a world where you went out to discos and there was a thing called a slow set, and if you were female you waited for a male to approach you and ask you to dance, which was basically code for 'Will you get off with me?' (in Dublin) or 'Do you fancy a shift?' (outside Dublin). After one or two songs and a snog, you'd nod awkwardly at each other and then walk away, possibly to never see each other again. Ah, the good old days.

We also went to pubs and chatted and flirted with people, and maybe you'd swap landline telephone numbers and maybe, just maybe, you'd go out on a date – although that was very American so probably not. You might meet at work (when that was still allowed) or a friend would introduce you to someone, or maybe you joined a club and met someone there. This all sounds so old-fashioned now, but it worked for millions of people. But nowadays it's all about online dating.

The chase

Online dating and apps were supposed to make dating easier, so why is it that so many single people cannot stand them? I think it comes down to 'the chase'. There is something in the chase that causes that *frisson*. But nowadays when you're online you have so much choice, you get to look at all these pics of women or men, and it's all a bit too easy. A date is organised, flirting is done and it's either move on to the sex stage or a thanks-but-no-thanks. It's all a bit unsexy, with zero chase involved.

Swipe up your life

People are genuinely sad about how meeting someone has been distilled down to a swipe. And while we have to admit that online dating is not something we have ever done, we like to think there are some real positives to it:

- You can widen your search and continue dating as you get older when the opportunities to socialise in pubs and clubs have dried up (or no longer interest you).
- You can specify your likes and dislikes to filter out time-wasters.
- You can go on multiple dates at your chosen venue.
- Online dating also allows for hook-ups – ones that you know won't come to anything except maybe a quick how's-your-father, and that's pretty great too.

I think when we take it too seriously, maybe that's when it all becomes too much. It's like going into a large supermarket to buy an apple. You go to the fruit and veg aisle and there are over 15 different types of apple. You start doubting yourself – you came in wanting a Pink Lady, but now the Granny Smith looks more appealing, or what about those fancy-looking organic ones? AAAGGGHHH! You end up running out of the supermarket and ringing your best friend, sobbing about apples, when what you should have done was pick up that first juicy-looking Pink Lady!

So how can you make online dating work for you?

I am going to start with the same advice that you've probably heard a million times from your parents, because it is the truth.

Just be yourself There is no point in pretending you love hiking, bungee jumping and surfing in Lahinch when in fact your preferred activities are pottering around town, eating cake and watching movies from the comfort of the couch.

Keep it natural Same goes for your profile pic — keep it natural and make sure it actually looks like you. You do not want a situation where you turn up on a date and they can't locate you because you don't look like yourself.

Coffee is a safe bet Keep the first date nice and simple — coffee is usually a safe bet. If it's going amazingly well, you can suggest a walk, but if it's going awfully you can knock back that espresso and say you've gotta dash. Nothing worse than being locked into a dinner on a first date and having to sit there, watching them eat chicken wings and licking every single one of their fingers every time they devour one (this actually happened to a friend of mine; we still laugh about 'chicken finger date').

Make an effort, but not too much You want to look like you've put in the effort, but not too much effort. Remember you are technically interviewing them ... it's not to see if they like YOU but if you like THEM. Although if they do like you and you also like them = winner!

And – finally – give them a chance This advice might make you feel 'the ick', but give them a chance. Humans are weird creatures and we can act bizarrely when in 'interview' situations. If you've genuinely had a bit of a laugh, enjoyed the chat and feel like you could continue the conversation then why not go for that second date? Even if you don't want to immediately rip their clothes off. Some of the greatest romances started as slow burns.

REMEMBER
YOU ARE
TECHNICALLY
INTERVIEWING
THEM ... IT'S
NOT TO SEE
IF THEY LIKE
YOU BUT
IF YOU
LIKE THEM.

There's someone for everyone

M **The dating landscape has changed dramatically since I was last in it. But like many of you reading this, I've had many a first date.**

- There was the one where he was mad into me but I wasn't into him at all and felt so bad (Catholic guilt, anyone?).
- There was the one where I was mad into him but all he talked about for the entire date was his ex-girlfriend. I felt like I was on a hidden camera show.
- There was the one who arrived completely pissed with his best friend in tow.
- There was the group date where I fancied someone other than the person I was supposed to be on the date with.
- There was the one where we clicked, but the timing was terrible.
- And, finally, there was the one I met through a friend (Jenny). We dated, we were a very slow burn … and now we're happily married!

So, if you're single and want to find love, keep going and stay in the arena. You will find your match and it will all have been worth it.

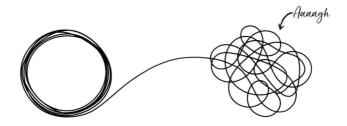

But why has dating become so complicated?

Why does dating nowadays seem to be some kind of mental gladiator exercise that you have to train for just to survive? Is it because everyone is so busy all the time with demanding jobs/careers? Is it because 'average' is no longer acceptable, and everyone must be exceptional? Or is it because everything is now based on a three-second glance at your face on an app?

Most of the brilliant, fab and funny single women I know work really hard all week, spend Saturday doing life admin, the laundry, shopping, cleaning the house, seeing their parents, meeting friends and getting ready for the coming week. Then Sunday night is spent swiping on whatever dating app they've chosen. There is so little time in their lives to actually go out and try to meet someone in real life. It's not easy out there!

Surviving the dating gladiator ring

Here are my tips on surviving in the gladiator ring of dating if you're still looking for the One.

- Don't give too much information away on the first date. It's supposed to be light and breezy and fun, an opportunity to see if there is enough common ground for a second date. We live in an age of oversharing and while watching *First Dates* on TV I'm frequently stunned at the level of personal information some daters give away. A first date is not the time to tell him or her about every personal trauma you've suffered.

- Focus on the chat, not the fact that he's wearing a shirt that you don't like (or that he has a ponytail! But Jenny disagrees with me on that).

- If the conversation flowed easily and you had a giggle, then it's a success.

- If you have children from a previous relationship, don't introduce them to a new partner too early. From personal experience I'd recommend waiting at least six months, or until you both know you're in this for the long haul.

- If you don't have children but are dating someone who does – see above point and be patient, be flexible and remember that they will always put their children first.

- No one is truly 'themselves' on a first date – not even you – so if sparks don't fly but you feel like you could continue the chat another time, then give them a second chance.

The perfect partner *and other mythical creatures*

Having realistic expectations when it comes to finding a partner is so important. I'm not saying you should settle for any aul pulse; however I've kept note of some real-life reasons that singletons I know (and love) have decided not to go on another date.

- 'He'd be lovely if he got rid of the ponytail.'
- 'He's 38 and can't drive.'
- 'He drove a red car, he made that choice himself.'
- 'He has a cat.'
- 'She bought a house on her own and you'd swear she was a property developer now.'
- 'I couldn't see her bogger accent in her photo on Tinder.'
- 'When I arrived he was drinking a short cocktail!'

Let's just look at all those reasons with different eyes. The 38-year-old who can't drive lives in Dublin City centre and doesn't need a car, the guy with a cat is a huge animal lover, the woman who bought a house on her own achieved something amazing considering the cost of living in this country right now. And the guy with the ponytail – you might even end up liking it!

Could it be that some singletons are standing in their own way, looking for a unicorn that doesn't exist? After all, at the end of the day, WE ARE ALL FLAWED.

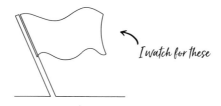

I watch for these

Red Flags

Having said all that, there are some genuine red flags to look out for when dating – here are mine.

- They are stingy. If a fuss is made about the bill, RUN. I may be old-fashioned, but I think it's OK to let the person who has asked you on the first date to pay, or to at least agree to split the bill without any fussing about who drank what or who ordered a side of chips.

- They don't ask you about you but love to talk about themselves. On a first date this may just be down to nerves, but if after a few dates they are still just yammering on about themselves … bye-bye.

- The relationship is catered entirely to their likes – e.g. they love Asian food so those are the only restaurants you go to.

- Your family events are not important to them.

- Negative comments are made often as 'jokes'.

- Their work/career is more important than yours.

- They are controlling – in the early stages of a relationship this could be something as simple as them ordering food for both of you in a restaurant.

- They want to move too fast in the relationship. Life is not a 400m sprint!

- They won't allow or don't like you having any alone time.

It's all about timing, this life!

I spent my 30th birthday with four very important women in my life; my two much older sisters (sorry, girls) and my dear friends Lynda and Jenny. I also spent a large part of the day crying. I was crying for lots of different reasons. On paper, my life was a mess; a broken marriage behind me, the journey of unravelling that legally ahead of me. I had a beautiful little boy who depended on me. Everyone around me was entering into the married phase of their lives and here I was exiting it, a failure. That brought me so much sadness. I was working way too much with two jobs, so I was really tired (cue more crying) and I was sure that there would be no time for me to meet someone else in my future. Even if I did want to meet anyone else it felt like it wasn't going to happen.

But it did... when I wasn't even looking.

Out with the old and in with the new

I believe that all previous relationships teach us lessons that we take with us to the next. I have learned who I am and what I really want from a relationship from being in ones that didn't work out. So, shout out to my exes — cheers, lads! That first flutter of excitement is intoxicating; seeing their name pop up on WhatsApp, getting ready to meet them for those early dates, matching all your bras and knickers. But that's just a moment in time and it all falls away eventually. This side of love is the one I love so much more. I love knowing everything there is to know. I love the realness of it. I love that there are no surprises (unless he actually plans to surprise me). The rock–solid nature of it.

This once–upon–a–time stranger (Louis) is the person I go to bed with and wake up with, spend all my free time with and, if all goes well, will continue to eat, sleep, and wake up with until one of us dies. That's our life plan.

But how do you know when you've met THE ONE?

- Our early dates in the first six months were all easy, free-flowing conversation and laughs.

- He was mature despite being five years younger than me. I got a lot of stick for this, but the slagging from others didn't kick off any negative chatter in my head.

- He was quietly confident in himself without ever being the loudest person in the room.

- I really fancied him (and I still do, 14 years on).

- He didn't ask questions about my previous relationship, but I knew if I wanted to talk about it I could and he wouldn't judge me.

- He listened to me (now he just listens to the podcast).

- I knew he would never intentionally hurt me and this made me feel safe. From early on I was sure that he was never going to pull the rug from under me.

- I trusted him completely (and still do).

- I was introduced to his lovely friends. You know that saying, 'Show me your friends and I'll tell you who you are'. Or, as it is in the Bible (yes, I'm quoting the Bible), 'The one who walks with the wise will become wise, but a companion of fools will suffer harm.'

- He showed me instead of told me. I was late to this advice from Maya Angelou: 'When people show you who they are, believe them the first time.' It's excellent advice for relationships – and for life in general.

Time spent with Louis was (and still is) easy. Each date we went on or phone conversation we had or night we spent together, I looked forward to the next one as soon as I was saying goodbye to him. That's the kind of relationship I've always wanted to be in — no drama, no regular conflict, just peaceful and fun.

It felt like a pressure-free zone, but maybe that's because our situation was quite unique. I was going through the long process of divorce, I already had a child and Louis was younger than me. So those annoying remarks of 'You're next', or 'Any sounds of wedding bells?' were never said to us. Without that external pressure, we were allowed to just … be.

I love being in love and the feeling of being loved in return is pure gold. I love making future plans with Louis, I love raising a family with him and I love doing all the boring, mundane tasks that a marriage, house, kids and pets involve with him.

Fourteen years on, and while some things have changed — like I wear heels less and Birkenstocks more (sorry Louis, thanks Jenny), we go out less and stay home with tea and Lindor chocolate truffles more — that iron-clad trust, respect, love and friendship is deeper than ever.

' **When people show you who they are,**

believe them the first time.

MAYA ANGELOU

,

The comfort zone

I I knew that I'd like the middle stage of being in a relationship. I was suited to the comfortable (some would say boring) phase of marriage.

You know that scene, you've seen it lots of times in a pub or restaurant, where a middle-aged couple are sitting opposite each other, not talking? I used to see them and cringe – *Oh my God, look at them, so bored of each other that they've nothing to say, I would die if that happened to me* – but of course, I had it wrong. That couple sitting there in comfortable silence are not performing for each other; they are at ease. They are comfortable in each other's company and nothing is forced. They are content.

'Content' is a bit of a dirty word – it sounds a bit like giving up. But it's a word I'd like to reclaim. It's like a Marks & Spencer fleece throw wrapped around you – it's cosy and comforting and warm. It's knowing that this person who you have shared so many years of your life with still likes you even though they know your maddest and darkest days. It's wanting to share something funny with them or talk through something that happened. It's wanting to just be with them, watching a TV show or sharing the same book (not at the same time, that would be weird). It's sitting together, eating dinner, talking and laughing or just being comfortably quiet. It's having a row and knowing that is not the end of the world. It's feeling safe.

Kindness beats excitement any day

A real relationship green flag for me is kindness. It's someone who makes you laugh, who thinks of you and cares for you. The person who thrills and excites you in your 20s and 30s is probably the exact person you would run screaming from when faced with a difficult or stressful situation, and guess what? There will be lots of those, because that's life.

Friendship first

If I were asked what, to me, is the most important thing in a relationship, I would say friendship. You have to be friends. Yes, we all hear about the early, butterflies-in-your-stomach stage, where it's all WHAM BAM, excitement and romance and fireworks. In a healthy relationship, this stage gradually passes and mellows out. We get comfortable and real, deep friendship and connection develops. In fact, if this stage doesn't pass, and if the infatuation causes anxiety and obsessive thoughts, this might not be love at all. It might be something called limerence.

The definition of limerence is 'a state of infatuation or obsession with another person that involves an all-consuming passion and intrusive thoughts' ... but this is not love. There is a difference. Limerence is almost an insanity and love is connection. What can happen for a lot of people who confuse love and limerence is that when they feel that intense early infatuation of a new relationship fading (which is normal), they panic and think that it means they are not with the right person and, more often than not, they finish with them. Only to desperately begin searching for the giddy height of limerence again with the next person.

When the infatuation stage passes, this is the perfect time to get real and honest about the relationship you are in and to see whether you have the foundations of a long-lasting relationship. This all sounds very mature and scientific and of course life is not like that, and we humans are certainly not like that when it comes to falling in love. I know that I was the limerence queen. I did not know it at the time as I had never even heard of the word, but I was very good at quickly becoming infatuated with someone before I even knew them properly. It didn't matter to me if it was not reciprocated – in fact, most of the time it was not – I would just decide that this person was AMAZING and that was all there was about it. Unfortunately for me (or fortunately, maybe) this meant that my failure rate was pretty consistent as there was no authentic connection there at all; it was as if I was playing at love.

And so, if you can call your partner your friend, then there is a real connection there. You not only love this person, you like them, you want to talk to them and spend time with them.

Myself and Ray talk all the time about everything and anything. Sitting at the kitchen counter drinking tea (me) and coffee (him), discussing the news stories of the day, how the kids are doing, a funny thing that happened, a new movie we might watch ... our friendship is the most important thing to me, and talking and sharing opinions and ideas is what makes our relationship strong and steady. And before you all start throwing your eyes to heaven, yes, of course we row and get annoyed with each other, but it's never so serious that it can't be solved by talking through it when we have both calmed down. I have learned this over the years – that talking to each other and keeping the lines of communication open will keep a relationship on track.

Tea fixes everything – well, almost.

And they all DIDN'T live happily ever after

M No one thinks, while selecting invitations for their wedding, that one day they might want to be so far away from their partner that they'll wish there was an apartment complex on Mars.

No one chooses a wedding venue and thinks that in the future they might be so mean to their spouse that they won't even recognise themselves.

Absolutely no one walks up the aisle arm in arm with their dad, looks at their partner, and thinks, 'One day we will be in the family courts getting a divorce.'

Because no one thinks their marriage will end ... yet in Ireland about 5,000 of them per year do. I know all this because mine was one of them.

We all want the fairytale, so ... once upon a time I was 22 and fell madly in love. I got engaged at 23, married at 24, had our son at 27, was separated at 29 and divorced at 34. The end.

So, what are the things I've learned about relationships since experiencing divorce? The beginning of a marriage is so full of hope, genuine love and unity. Whereas its ending is filled with a lot of stress, sadness and division.

We often hear that buying and moving house is the most stressful thing you'll ever do. I've moved house six times and would move again tomorrow. But ending a marriage is possibly the most difficult decision one can make in a lifetime and it's a very painful process to go through, too.

Of course, there are the obvious reasons for a break-up such as domestic abuse or infidelity, but in my opinion, the majority of marriage break-ups happen because of three reasons.

1. Repetitive disappointment This is death by 10,000 tiny cuts or 10,000 little let-downs. It's a feeling that something is off but it isn't big enough to mention, let alone worth having an argument over.

It might be a text that goes unanswered, a hand not held, a negative remark made as a 'joke' in front of others, a broken promise to help more with the kids. As standalone incidents go they are not a problem, but over time constant disappointment turns into resentment. Then that resentment turns to anger, and when we are angry we are not the best versions of ourselves. No one wants to hang out with the person they're angry with, never mind be intimate with them. And then *that* becomes another problem.

2. Poor communication If you can't speak together you won't sleep together. No marriage ends on a Thursday night in April after just one argument, but that argument could be *the one* where someone says, 'Enough, I'm done.' And that will eventually happen if there is poor communication. If one partner doesn't listen, or always seems distracted when the other is speaking, or uses the silent treatment as a form of punishment, then the relationship has communication issues that need addressing.

There is a great example of this in the 2006 film *The Break-Up*, starring Jennifer Aniston and Vince Vaughn. Aniston's character Brooke is hosting a family dinner party, and she asks Gary (Vince Vaughn) to buy 12 lemons on his way home from work. He swans in, grabs a beer from the fridge, flicks on the TV and flings a bag her way in the kitchen. Inside the bag are three lemons – nine lemons short of what she asked for. Later on, the lack of lemons leads to a humongous argument that Gary didn't see coming. They both shout and roar and offend one another. They say things that have obviously been bothering both of them for months. That row ultimately leads to the end of their relationship. Watching this film some years after I was divorced, I felt that scene demonstrated really well how the majority of break-ups happen. It's never about the lemons. It's about ALL the unsaid stuff that builds up and then blasts out like a volcano spewing red-hot insults ... and that, my friends, is not the best way to communicate with someone who you are in a relationship with – ever.

3. Lack of compatibility You need to be friends. Simply put, a relationship will end when there are just too many differences. I'm not talking about how he loves true crime podcasts and you like to watch endless home renovation shows – we all need our individual interests too, of course. I'm talking about the lack of compatibility that was always there but that you chose to overlook, thinking it was a case of 'opposites attract'. These are differences on big issues, such as dissimilar approaches to problem-solving, different parenting styles or when your life values don't align. And when you struggle to find common ground on any niggling issue, you will get to a place where you wonder how you ever said, 'I do'. Because the baseline for a good marriage is being friends, the best of friends. And if you're not compatible you cannot be comrades.

Even though a marriage break-up takes its toll on your physical health (I had a frequent upset tummy) and your mental health (I did not sleep properly for a year), when we arrived at the decision to end things there was a huge sense of relief for both of us. Up until then I felt so much extreme sadness, shame and embarrassment. I was heartbroken and felt like a failure, and all the while like I was holding my breath, too. It was nice to feel like I could finally exhale. However, this was temporary, because the decision to end things is only the beginning of a new journey – one that you unfortunately can't navigate with the help of Google Maps.

The best way to describe a marriage break-up

A marriage break–up is like one of those huge, ugly red spots you get on your face *(that's all the fighting)*, you know the ones that are deep under the skin and throb with pain *(more disagreements)*, and then finally after what feels like forever a big yellow head appears on it. Yes! You can finally squeeze it, and you do *(that's the decision to end the marriage)*. Relief at last … but afterwards you're left with an open wound, and you know that it is definitely going to scar *(that's divorce)*.

I do still have some emotional scars, albeit small ones. But I learned a lot about myself and my own resilience. I also realised that whatever the situation, no relationship breaks down because of just one person. And despite all the anguish I have no regrets, because before my marriage ended there was lots of love and so many happy times, too. And as a result of that relationship I have one of the greatest loves of my life, my son Dara.

Advice – if you want it, read on

- Don't get married in your 20s. You haven't got enough lived experience to deal with the possible (definite) stresses that may arise. You need those 10 years of work, travel, dating other people and living alone to know who YOU really are before entering into a marriage.

- This may sound obvious but make sure the relationship is really over before exiting – try counselling, either couples or solo, before you decide to end a marriage. If you do this, it means you can really move on and live the rest of your life in peace with zero regrets and no 'what if's.

- This one will be hard, but try to take the emotion out of the process and take a more practical approach, especially if there are children involved. Their wellbeing is paramount, and while you might not love their mum or dad anymore, remember that they still do and always will.

- You will need professional advice from a family law solicitor, but note that each letter they send or phone call they take will cost you. The average cost of a divorce in Ireland is between €10,000 and €20,000, and each spouse must pay their own costs, so less back and forth means a less expensive outcome.

- What would you say to your best friend if they were going through a divorce? Say that advice out loud to yourself. I did this, and it helped me on many occasions. Let go of any resentment – by doing this you will be kinder to yourself.

- Finally, always keep in mind that this, too, shall pass.

What we know now about →

weddings

OR, WHY YOU SHOULD NEVER LISTEN TO ANYONE ELSE'S ADVICE AND JUST DO WHAT YOU WANT TO DO

The wedding formula

J What could be nicer than sharing a day filled with love and matrimony with a couple making a public declaration of their commitment to each other? By the time you get to our age you have been to a LOT of weddings and the majority of them have followed the same formula: church ceremony, followed by the dash to the pub for a quick drink, head to the venue for the reception and then dinner (beef or salmon) followed by deranged dancing till at least 2 a.m. Fun!

But in the last few years things have changed quite a lot – people have realised that they don't have to do it the way it has always been done and have started looking at alternatives. We're not talking about the couples who go deep–sea diving to take their vows or jump out of airplanes – we mean the couples who decide that they want a smaller wedding, a different type of ceremony, or the very brave who elope and come home shouting, 'SURPRISE!'

Taking the time to really figure out what you want for your day takes strength because, believe me, EVERYONE is going to have an opinion. When we worked on the radio together, we knew that if we mentioned the word 'wedding' we would get lots and lots of emails and text messages into the show. It is the one thing that pretty much everyone has an opinion on: how big or small it should be, who to invite or not to invite, where to have it, what to eat, wear, dance to, etc. With three weddings between us, here's what we know now about the wedding minefield!

Throw this later

Saying yes to a dress is tricky

(M) Okay, so you've done the dating, you've decided you're compatible – it's time to settle down. As you already know, I've had two weddings. But what you won't know is that I hated both my wedding dresses. Yes, BOTH.

I never got the fuzzy wuzzy feelings when shopping for a wedding dress, because I didn't enjoy the process. The first time I went dress shopping the Celtic tiger was roaring all over Dublin. I ran into a shop to have a look one day while on my lunch break and the lady informed me that it was by appointment only. 'Okay, sure,' I said, 'can I come in on Saturday?' They didn't have a Saturday appointment for over three months, and the wedding was six months away.

Eventually I got to try on some gowns and I HATED all of them. Fishtail was particularly gick on me, ballgown made me look like a wannabe Belle. A-line, fit and flare, square neckline, halter neck, jewels or no jewels – aaaagh! I didn't like any of them!

In one store I wandered over to the bridesmaid section and picked up a strapless sweetheart dress in lilac (and at 24 years old my boobs were great, so strapless was a good option then). I tried it on, it fit, I looked like myself, I could move and I didn't feel like I was carrying 12kg of fabric and beads. I decided this was the best of a bad bunch and ordered it in white ... but love it? I'm not sure I even liked it.

Ten years later I was engaged again and shopping for a wedding dress once more. And while I was so excited to marry Louis, I *hated* shopping for the dress. I found it even more intimidating, more confusing and more stressful than the first time.

Not once did I try on a dress and think, 'Wow, I love this.' But time was running out and I needed to make a choice, so I went with a plain, plain, plain white dress, V–necked at the front and back, fitted at the waist, with a full A–line skirt. One thing I did like was that it had pockets. Really handy for my lippy all day and somewhere to put my hands in all the photos. I didn't love the dress (it's currently rolled up in a ball under our bed), but I do love the husband I sleep beside each night, and that's what really matters.

The dos and don'ts

So, with two weddings under my belt, here are my dos and don'ts for a stress–free event:

- Elope... but if that's not an option, read on.
- Shop alone for the first month to see what YOU like before you take anyone else along.
- If you are going for a big wedding and are humming and hawing about inviting Auntie Noleen, invite her. About 10 per cent of guests will drop out before the big day and a potential row with Auntie Noleen is not worth the hassle.
- If you are having a two-day event, don't invite everyone who has been to the wedding to come along to day two. Keep that just for those who you and your partner are really close to.
- Take fewer posed photos and more candid ones – they are always the best and won't interrupt your day as much.
- You don't have to have 'official' bridesmaids – just have your bestie or sister wear whatever they want and ask them to help you throughout the day.
- Both Ray and Louis disagree with this, but get a videographer. It would be so nice now to watch it back with the kids and see and hear the voices of people we have lost since the wedding.

What's the alternative?

J When Ray and I decided to get married, we did it kind of backwards — as in, we had kids first, bought a house together and then made it official. So, when it came to the actual ceremony, we knew that we wanted to stand up in front of all the friends and family who'd been there with us along the way and declare our commitment and love to each other. As much as I dreamt about eloping it just didn't seem right, and so it was us and 120 of our loved ones all together for our humanist ceremony in Tankardstown House in Co. Meath.

When it came to choosing my dress, I did that on my own. I did go wedding dress shopping one day with my two bridesmaids, but nothing sparks fear in my heart like shopping and trying on clothes with others. I hate it. I want to be on my own, taking my time to feel how I feel in the dress. And it is a cliché, but after LOTS of trying on, when I eventually put on my platinum Jenny Packham dress (with sleeves, of course), I just knew it was the one. I loved my dress.

The day itself couldn't have been better. The sun shone, Ray surprised me by asking Declan O'Rourke to sing one of my favourite songs, 'Galileo', at our wedding ceremony. After saying our 'I Do's, Ray, carrying baby Tom, and Kate and I holding hands all walked down the aisle together, beaming. Later that evening, Ray and Kate surprised me with a choreographed dance sequence to 'How Sweet It Is To Be Loved By You' by Marvin Gaye. They had secretly gone to dance classes together. We had 'Elvis: The Way it Was' as our wedding band which led to a massive dance–off between the guests that I will remember forever. We stayed up till 5 a.m. singing, dancing and laughing, on the biggest high. It really was one of my favourite days ever.

BUT, if I was getting married tomorrow it would look very different indeed. It would be tiny, as in, fewer than ten people there. I would wear a fab suit, I would get married in a registry office in Dublin and then walk down to a lunch venue for a gorgeous meal and then be home later that evening. I'd then head off on a fab holiday with my family the next day and think about how gorgeous the whole thing was.

Isn't that mad? It's the total opposite to my actual wedding, but that's what happens after 11 years of marriage — you realise that all the hoo-ha doesn't make the wedding. It really all comes down to you and your partner (and children if you have them already). And yes, I know that if we had done it that way, we would probably have upset people, but what I've learned is that it's OK to upset people. Adults can handle being upset or disappointed.

So, in conclusion, my advice for a happy big day, having gone through it all and attended a gazillion weddings?

Don't listen to anyone's advice and just do what you want to do.

The End.

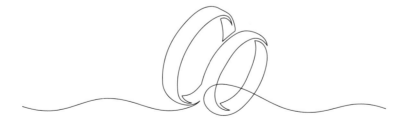

DON'T LISTEN TO ANYONE'S ADVICE AND JUST DO WHAT YOU WANT TO DO.

THE END.

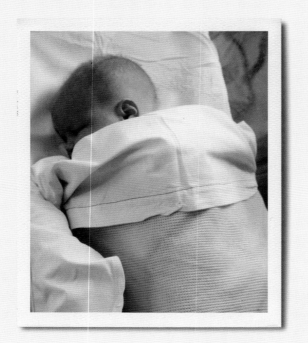

What we know now about ↘

motherhood

OR, HOW LIFE HAS PLANS FOR YOU THAT YOU KNOW VERY LITTLE ABOUT

If it's supposed to be so natural, then why is it so hard?

J   Even though I was pregnant for nine months, I hadn't really thought about the days and weeks to follow when I would actually have a physical baby in my arms. I didn't know too much about babies; I liked them, but not in the way I'd seen other women go crackers over a newborn. But I was sure once my baby arrived, I'd just know what to do.

Well, ha–bloody–ha!

I could not have imagined that the day after giving birth to my first child, I would be sitting up in bed crying, with two nappies soaked in warm water wrapped around both my breasts. The midwife had told me it would ease the pain after my milk came in, and it did ease that pain, but not the ever-growing anxiety I was feeling inside. I was determined to breastfeed my baby. I tried to get her to latch on and failed, tried again and failed. Each time baby Kate was getting more distressed as she was hungry, and I was getting tense and upset. If this was supposed to be so natural, then why was it so hard? I was not prepared for this, or the tiredness. I had laboured and then eventually ended up having an emergency C-section. I was wiped out, and yet my anxiety was keeping me awake and hypervigilant.

I left the hospital feeling shell-shocked.

I wondered why no one could tell me exactly what to do and how to look after this little life. I kept hearing that I'd figure it out, that I'd feel my way around it. I remember a woman looking into the pram to have a gawk at baby Kate and she said, 'Oh lucky you, lots of Christmas cuddles on the couch,' and I didn't understand what she meant because I could not imagine relaxing on a couch with a baby! I felt a low-level panic and fear. And I was crying – a lot. And I am not a crier. To put it into context, the last time I'd had a roaring, sobbing cry was in 2011. So, this crying was not normal for me. Was it baby blues or something else? I'm not sure because I didn't tell anyone. I don't tend to ask for help; I always think I can figure things out for myself. So, I did what I always do – I looked to books. I eventually found one that clicked with me; it was no nonsense and gave me a routine I desperately needed and could follow because, right then, I did not trust my own instincts.

The book told me to wake my baby an hour before I'd have to leave the house when I eventually went back to work, so I woke Kate up at 6 a.m. I am actually cringing typing this, thinking, 'Why, oh why, would I wake a sleeping baby?' I'd bring her downstairs in the dark (it was December) and feed her. Then there would be 'awake time' until another feed and then nap time ... repeat throughout the day, always putting the baby down to sleep in a darkened room. No matter what, my rule was: DO NOT DEVIATE FROM THE ROUTINE. I remember my sister asking me to come meet her for coffee with the baby and I was horrified. Leave the house? But what about the routine?

The pressure I was putting myself under was ridiculous. Ray was back at work, and I was left alone, unable to relax even when Kate was sleeping as I was ticking off lists of things I had to do and would have to do later.

And did I mention the relentless breastfeeding? The sore nipples and trying to figure out if Kate was getting enough milk. I locked myself away for that first month, didn't really see anyone and thought to myself that this was obviously how most women felt after having a baby, but that no one spoke about it.

And then one morning when I was in bed, Ray got up before me and, instead of me getting up with the baby, he handed Kate to me in bed and I fed her there. She was all warm and cosy beside me, and I was smiling looking at her beautiful, tiny face, and she was cooing up at me, and Ray slipped off to work and then something magical happened: we both fell back asleep in bed together until later that morning. It was heaven. And I remember thinking, 'Oh, this might be better than the getting-up-at-6-a.m. lark and keeping to an army regime'. And so it began that I very slowly began to relax into this new motherhood phase of my life.

And it was a wonderful, messy, anxiety-inducing, sleep-deprived time. And that is the thing about becoming a first-time mother — it is all those things. It is not Instagram-perfect — it couldn't be because it is life, in all its messy, mad ways. Someone once said to us that it would be the steepest learning curve of our lives and I have to agree. Nothing I have ever done before or since comes near the feeling of becoming a first-time parent. But it does get easier, and you do find your way.

From that first moment that I held Kate and stared into her eyes I knew that she would be one of my deepest loves. All I could think about was the huge responsibility of minding this newborn, magical being, when in fact she was the one teaching and changing me. And so it continues to this day, 17 years later. And just to prove the extreme learning curve that is parenting, when baby Tom arrived five-and-a-half years later, it was a totally different experience. I felt like Mother Earth. I was very relaxed and at ease. I trusted my mothering skills and went with the flow. I had no routine with him and he slept in our bed. I was very confident in my ability to mind this new little baby and it felt wonderful, which was helped by his being a very chilled-out baby. (Or was that because I was so relaxed? Who knows?)

IT IS NOT
INSTAGRAM-
PERFECT —
IT COULDN'T
BE BECAUSE
IT IS LIFE,
IN ALL ITS
MESSY,
MAD WAYS.

Some advice, if I may

Just in case you are reading this while pregnant, I would like to give some advice (I realise you might have a pain in your arse with unwanted advice, but this might give you something to think about):

Ask for practical help where possible I remember putting Kate in her bouncer in the bathroom while I took a shower, not able to properly wash myself as I was so preoccupied with keeping an eye on her. Ask a family member to watch the baby so you can take some time to look after yourself.

Breastfeeding is hard I wish someone had told me this truth. I presumed I'd just be able to do it. I had to work very hard to get it to work, but when it did eventually click, I found it was the best thing for both of us. It was such a bonding experience and gave us both a lot of time together, sitting and cuddling. It forces you to stop and take that time. If you want to do it, then I'd suggest looking for support from a lactation consultant. I didn't do this and think it could have made my life a hell of a lot easier if I had.

Your partner should be the gatekeeper to your house for the first month No unwanted visitors; in fact, I'd say keep visitors to the very minimum. People are dying to meet the baby but whatever it is about being an Irish woman, you will start fussing over them and making sure the guest is looked after. This is not what you need that first month. You need to be minded and allowed to rest and the baby is getting settled into its new home. So, trust me, keep visitors at bay.

Time will feel slow initially, then will go into super-speed Before you know it you will be back in work, so allow yourself the time to just enjoy being together. Don't worry about your messy house. You will never get this special time back with your baby. You will look back upon it like a dream. And before you know it you will be looking at a 17-year-old near-adult, thinking, 'How did that happen?'

Talk to someone If you feel how I felt, anxious and overwhelmed, talk to someone. If I could go back in time and be my own best friend, I'd tell myself that tears are normal and feeling anxious is normal too. For some reason we don't tend to share our negative stories, so there is a presumption that becoming a mum is all Disney-like and joyous. It's not always like that, and that's normal too. You are finding your way and so is your new baby. Be kind to yourself and take any help offered. And just on those anxious feelings: mine went away after a few weeks, but for some new mums the anxiety remains or gets worse. It's really important that you talk to someone and tell them how you are feeling. There is lots of support out there. Do not suffer in silence. You will be OK.

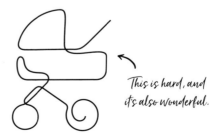

This is hard, and it's also wonderful.

'Have ye got tender breasts?'

M I walked into a Dublin City centre pharmacy directly across the road from Today FM and asked for a pregnancy test. The young girl behind the counter was a true–blue Dub and said, very loudly, 'Have ye got tender breasts?' I quietly said, 'Em, yes, I think so.' Then she followed up with, 'Ahhh, come here, it's not the end of the world if ye are!'

Jenny, whose laugh is far from discreet, was with me and she ran for the door howling. For the rest of the day, she kept rubbing her chest in the office and mouthing 'tender breasts' at me.

I took the test at home, and it showed up positive in a nanosecond. No need for the 3–minute wait time. I was definitely pregnant, and I was over the moon. Apart from almost 16 weeks of morning sickness that lasted ALL day, that first pregnancy was easy … but then, I was only 26.

On Easter Monday 2007, in the middle of a nurses' strike, my beautiful baby boy Dara came into the world and *my world* changed forever. I know for so many the arrival of their first baby is a total shock. The lack of sleep, coupled with the recovery from either vaginal or C-section birth, all while minding and feeding a tiny human, is an enormous undertaking. But I was so lucky that I was given a little baby boy who fed instantly and slept all the time. Dara was the easiest baby – in fact, he was almost always like a tiny adult. And I can't take any credit because I hadn't a clue what I was doing. Now, 17 years later, he's still the same – he loves his food and his sleep (and his mum). And I can honestly say I've learned far more from Dara than he ever did or will from me.

Returning to the real world post-baby

Even as someone who loved my job, I dreaded going back to work. I was in a lovely love bubble with Dara. We had our daily routine and work was just going to get in the way of it. But the return date was sitting there just waiting for me as he was now 11 months old – yes, I had managed to squeeze every last day out of maternity leave by sticking holidays onto the end of unpaid leave. I'd done everything you're supposed to do to get ready – if you're planning the post–baby return to work yourself, here's what you need to think about.

Organise great childcare (good luck with that) This started off with the great 'creche or childminder' debate. I decided that a childminder was a more flexible fit for us, but a great one is not easy to find. I put an ad on a parenting website and got many replies and one of those replies was from Kay. We are still working together all these years later. She's the closest thing to Mary Poppins I've met, but without the big bag.

Try to ease yourself back in I started leaving Dara with Kay once or twice a week in the month leading up to my return to work. If it's at all possible, go back to work on a Wednesday so your first week back is short. You can see the weekend just ahead.

Start getting your head back into work mode Make sure you're up to date on what's happening in your workplace. It took me over a month to fire up to full speed again. Returning to work after maternity leave is physically and mentally exhausting because you're trying to focus fully on your job while there and then be a present parent when at home.

Still, even with all the prep done, leaving Dara with another woman every day felt so unnatural and I hated it. But I didn't have a choice.

My one and only?

When my first marriage ended, I did a great job of convincing myself and others that Dara would be my one and only. I adored him so much, but I felt like the chances of me having another child were zilch. I was over 30, waiting for my divorce to go through, and I felt that by the time I'd be ready to meet someone new I'd be at least 40.

Life has plans for you that you know very little about

And yet, nine years after my first baby was born, I was pregnant again. I was beaming with happiness and felt so lucky to get to experience this again. Everything was so different this time; I had no morning sickness (yippee), I was older, wiser and calmer, and I knew from looking at my little man Dara that it flies by, so I wanted to enjoy every minute of this special time. My long-legged lady Eliza was born in September. This tiny beauty that I never thought I'd have was finally here in my arms. Immediately anyone with eyes could see that she was the head off her father (but she's got my personality).

Bonnie arrived less than two years later. She's our beautiful brown-eyed girl with a fully formed American accent. Eliza and Bons became best friends the moment they met.

I've always felt that my younger children have really benefited from the age gap between them and their big brother. Dara has been a constant marker of time in my life; I feel like I haven't changed, but he continues to grow taller and older and has moved through school years in a flash. His presence constantly reminds me of how time moves too quickly. On those dark, hazy nights of relentless breastfeeding with either Eliza or Bonnie, I had the wisdom to know that this madness would pass, this tiredness would lift and soon, little one, you'll be on your feet, so I'm going to enjoy this time with only us two awake.

Sometimes a welcome and happy pregnancy doesn't result in a baby

More than one in five pregnancies ends in miscarriage, which affects around 14,000 women in Ireland each year. I'm never sure what the correct term to use is. Should I say I experienced a miscarriage, I suffered a miscarriage, I had a miscarriage, or I lost a pregnancy (which always sounds careless to me ... like, I've lost so many lip liners)?

So, I'll say: I've had three miscarriages.

In the weeks after I finished breastfeeding Eliza, I discovered I was pregnant again. I was on cloud nine with this news — I felt great, Eliza was thriving and having a sibling so close in age was going to be a bonus. I was three days away from shooting a new series of *Getaways*, the travel show that I worked on at the time. As usual, I needed to pick up a few bits in town for the trip. My dad came along to push Eliza in her pram, which meant I could zip in and out of the shops and get the job done in half the time. We picked up all the things I needed then headed home to collect Dara from school. While walking around earlier in the day I'd had mild tummy pains but nothing I was concerned about. But at home later that afternoon, as I was making us all some sandwiches, the cramps became quite painful. They were in my stomach and then also moved down into my thighs ... and then, suddenly, I felt wet. *Fuck, fuck, fuck, no ... please don't be what I think this is.* I calmly handed Dad tea and a sandwich and went to the bathroom. I was bleeding heavily. Louis and I still hadn't told anyone that I was pregnant again, so I made up a ridiculous excuse, which was, 'Oh no, Dad, I totally forgot I've booked a beauty appointment. Can you stay here and mind Dara? I'll take Eliza with me.' Dad, always ready to lend a hand, said of course he could stay.

I quickly changed into black leggings, packed a little bag and flagged a taxi on the road. My head was saying it was gone, but my heart was hoping it would hang on in there.

The ultrasound was clear... no tiny wriggle on screen, no heartbeat, an empty sac. It wasn't meant to be. My Christmas baby was 'lost'.

But like so many women who have experienced this, I just got on with things. Three days later, I flew to Transylvania for work armed with pads and painkillers.

The fourth baby

I've always wanted four children. Does 'want' make me sound greedy? I'm from a family of three girls and growing up I always thought one more would have evened things out. Louis was on board with my number too.

After Bonnie was born, Professor Malone in the Rotunda asked me, 'Well, Mairéad, will I be seeing you again?' I said, 'Yes, absolutely, I'll be done when I have four.' That was the plan. Plans are great until you can't get them off the ground.

During Covid, when it seemed every female on the planet of Instagram was getting pregnant, I wasn't. I couldn't understand why. After having three children naturally, I was now getting fertility tests done. The results showed that the issue lay with me. I had just turned 40 and the odds were stacked against me. After what felt like a long time sitting on a waiting list, we finally got in for fertility treatment.

Although I know lots of couples who have gone down the IVF route, I really didn't know a whole lot about it until I went through it too. There's a lot of poking, prodding, testing, scanning and drug–taking involved. When you collect your meds from the pharmacy you look like you've done a massive shopping haul with multiple bags. Oh, and there's a bin too, for disposing of the needles.

I went into Today FM each day, did the radio show, got home, made dinner, got the kids to bed, got drugs from the fridge, cleaned the tummy area with an alcohol wipe, then Louis attached the needle to the pen and I stuck it into a chosen spot near my belly button.

This secret ritual created severe bloating, to the point where after just 14 days I didn't own a pair of trousers or jeans that fit. The irony of looking pregnant when you are certainly not is really frustrating. But I didn't suffer from any of the other side effects such as fatigue, breast tenderness, mood swings, or abdominal pain. So, I thought, 'This is easy.' (Ha!)

IVF is just a numbers game

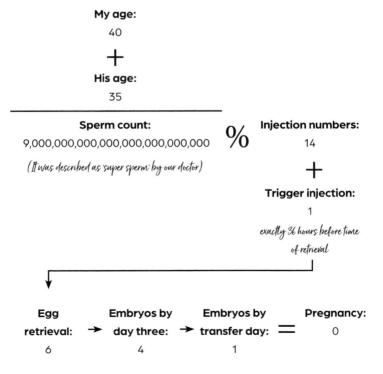

My age:
40

+

His age:
35

Sperm count:
9,000,000,000,000,000,000,000,000

(It was described as 'super sperm' by our doctor)

%

Injection numbers:
14

+

Trigger injection:
1

exactly 36 hours before time of retrieval

Egg retrieval:
6
→
Embryos by day three:
4
→
Embryos by transfer day:
1
=
Pregnancy:
0

Because I didn't have a rough time physically, I wanted to do it again. This time they suggested changing the medication. Same routine: get the kids to bed, inject the fertility drug, try to relax and go to bed. And then do it all again tomorrow. But this round felt so different. I was FLOORED. Extreme fatigue, breasts so tender they felt bruised, headaches, moods that changed like the Irish weather and severe bloating – the kind that makes you look like you're about five months pregnant.

Back to the numbers again: 6 eggs retrieved, same as last time.

And then the waiting.

Waiting for the call to say how many eggs have become embryos.

Waiting for the next call to say how many embryos survived.

Willing these little things to hang on in there: *I promise I will look after you so well. I'm a good baby cooker.'*

One embryo made it to day five. Transfer day was a sunny Sunday morning, which was great, as it's the only easy time to find parking in Dublin City centre.

It was done in minutes, and we left and hoped for every minute of the next 14 days.

I knew by the 'Hello' of the lovely nurse who called. I knew for sure by the tone of her voice when she said, 'Can you confirm your name and date of birth?' Even as I was doing that, I knew she was going to use the word 'unsuccessful'.

No fourth baby.

Que será, será

Whatever will be, will be

The future's not ours to see

Que será, será

I'm a mother of three. They have unlocked a love that I didn't know was in me; a wholly unconditional love that belongs only to them. When we are together I feel as though I have everything.

The thing about motherhood is, I'm still learning with each passing year. Baby phase — learning (or surviving), toddler stage — learning, teen years — LEARNING! In the not-too-distant future, I'll have an adult child, as Dara turns 18 in 2025 — more learning for me.

I'll leave you with my favourite mum quote:

'If at first you don't succeed, try doing it the way mum told you to in the first place!'

Motherhood is a state of being

I Over the years I've seen some female friends lose babies through miscarriage, others grieve not having children they very much wanted because they did not meet the right person, and others who made the decision that having a child was not for them. I know women who have gone it alone with the help of a sperm donor and friends dealing with fertility issues after having one, two or three babies. I've met women grieving stillborn babies and babies who could not survive because of life-limiting conditions. Each of these women has her own story to tell, but at the core of all these stories is a woman who has had to come to some sort of peace with whatever tragedy has happened or whatever decision has been made. And as far as I can see, that peace does come. It doesn't mean that whatever pain and sadness you might experience will disappear, more that they are subsumed within and become part of who you are. What makes you who you are.

And I really believe that the term 'mother' covers such a varied and wide range of possible meanings that there is no one way of defining it. We all were mothered and we all can find ourselves mothering even without having our own biological children. It's a state of being, a natural female caring response — for family members, friends in need and our beloved pets. To be female is to mother, and for the most part we should be mothering ourselves, guiding ourselves through this sometimes-difficult life. As much as we want to be our own best friend, it's just as important to mother ourselves too — in the times when we know that an early night is best for us, or that we shouldn't be with that person who makes us feel 'less than'. This knowing is mothering in the truest sense of the word.

TO BE FEMALE
IS TO MOTHER,
AND FOR
THE MOST
PART WE
SHOULD BE
MOTHERING
OURSELVES.

A trip to teenager-land

(M) I once got some good advice from another mum who at the time had two teens. She said, 'Mairéad, put a photograph of Dara on the fridge of a time when he's really cute — say, age 9. Your child at that age believed you knew everything, they wanted hugs, kisses and tuck–ins at night. Because when they are 14 you'll need to be reminded often that that little boy is still in there somewhere.'

They come out the other side eventually, albeit much taller, with a completely different voice and an appetite that needs a second mortgage to satisfy. So here's what I know now about parenting teens (very little).

Pick your battles The constant 'clean up your room' nagging will become nothing more than background noise, so leave it and just close the door. Their room = their space, but everywhere else in the home they should pick up and clean up after themselves instantly.

Don't only have conversations about school Sometimes parents only talk to their teens about school, tests and teachers. It's the equivalent of only talking to a friend about work — it's boring. So stop it.

They will flit between having high expectations and low self-esteem Expect mood swings and try your best not to overreact — they usually pass.

Be a house plant Teens need to know you are always there, but they don't want you to interfere, so sometimes you need to act like a house plant. Just be present in the room, looking pretty and cleaning the air.

Listen on the double, talk on the single You have two ears and one mouth for a reason. Sometimes the best conversations with your teen will involve you smiling and nodding. I find 'uh-hmmm' or some equivalent agreeing sound is good.

Teach them to cook the basics It's a lovely thing to do with teens and also gives them responsibility for feeding themselves as they move from being a child into adulthood. It's also handy when they want to eat something different (I hate cooking two dinners).

Stop trying to fix everything for your teen When my six-year-old is upset I use distraction, hugs, a game or an episode of *Bluey* to soothe her. With teens we tend to want to jump in and 'fix' the problem. But it's at this stage (and it's easier said than done) where we need to take a little step back and help them to help themselves figure out the situation and fix the problem.

Be their friend I know as a parent it's hard to be both a friend and a parent sometimes, but during the teenage years there are times where you will need to 'act' like a friend. That doesn't mean saying 'yeah bro' to everything they want to do — boundaries are still necessary — but this is a time when the most important thing to them is their friends, so be one too.

Remember you don't own them — you just have them on loan Freedom for a 13-year-old looks very different to freedom for a 17-year-old. So teens need age-appropriate freedom, and they need to begin to make decisions for themselves, by themselves. They need to make mistakes and they need to be trusted while doing all of that too. Going through the years, I've found this to be the hardest part because all I want to do is bubble-wrap him and keep him safe, but then that wouldn't allow him to flourish.

What we know now about →

being human

OR, WHY YOU NEED TO PUT DOWN YOUR PHONE

Growing a sense of OK-ness

J I've always been very interested in psychology and what makes the human mind tick. What makes people the way they are? Is it nature or nurture? Who knows what anyone else is really feeling? We should all probably be going to therapy. Human beings need to process past hurts in order to live good lives. If we ignore the past, we do so at our peril; it will always find a way to come out, whether it's through overworking, emotional eating, failed relationships, people-pleasing, anger issues, narcissism, sadness or depression. I went to therapy back in 2019. I had been thinking about it for some time, and when I eventually got up the nerve I found it to be a really positive experience. It took some time for me to relax into the situation and stop myself from performing, but once I did I managed, with the therapist's help, to get clarity on a lot of things in my life.

Say hello to your feelings

One simple step we can all take is to acknowledge our feelings when we feel them first arising. This has been a huge lesson for me. I used to react to situations, believing that I was simply reacting to what had just happened or what had just been said. I realise now that it was a whole lot deeper than that. A lot of our reactions are conditioned from childhood hurts.

For example, I can get quite stressed when we are all heading off somewhere as a family. I'll start panicking everyone and shouting about coats and scarfs and dogs and what we might forget, and Jesus Christ, where are my shoes? By the time we get in the car I have made everyone stressed.

So, I thought about what is triggered in me and why I act this way, and remembered a time in my youth when these exact situations would stress me out. I didn't like that panicked feeling as a child but I was recreating it as an adult. Once I examined the feeling and named it, it became easier to recognise it when it began building up in me. Now when I notice it, I stop and say hello to the feeling, 'Ah, there you are,' and by acknowledging it, I am able to calm myself down (well, most of the time).

Recognising your triggers is crucial in helping with stress. I'm not suggesting that I'm going around all calm and Zen-like all the time (my kids would have something to say about that) but I do know that I am so much better for recognising the feelings inside me. It's like a little warning light flickering, letting me know that if I don't acknowledge it, it will grow in me and eventually explode.

The modern world does not suit us

Again and again, we are told that the way the modern world is designed does not suit us. We have lost our connection with ourselves, with others and with the natural world. And it is not our fault, but it does mean that we have to take back some control and find out all the ways that we can mind our mental health before that choice is taken out of our hands. I don't want this to sound like a Pollyanna version of 'how to be happy'. I am not talking here about people who have clinical depression and are, I hope, in the hands of specialised doctors and taking any medication that may be necessary to help them on their path to wellness. I am talking about those of us who are stressed by this modern world and who are probably not taking the time to mind ourselves. There are daily things that we can do that have huge benefits for our general wellbeing. It's not about feeling happy all the time – that is impossible. It's about growing a general sense of OK-ness.

Things to help you grow in contentment and enjoy day-to-day life

Get outdoors for a walk every day Whether it's long or short, and whether you do it with your headphones in, listening to a podcast, or with nothing in your ears except the sound of nature, it doesn't matter – just get outside.

Lift weights This does not mean that you have to go to the gym. I have a yoga mat and some dumbbells I use at home. There are lots of people online to follow for inspiration, which is particularly helpful when you're starting out. Always start with a very low weight and build up gradually. With repetition and consistency you start feeling your muscles grow and your strength building, and there is no better feeling.

Get at least eight hours of sleep a night Controversial suggestion: do not have a TV in your bedroom. I know it's lovely to be all cosy and warm in bed and to be able to switch on your favourite TV show, but I think for the best sleep hygiene you should not have one in there. The light and noise from a TV are very disruptive to sleep and your bedroom should be a calm haven of peace. Why not try an experiment for 30 days and make your bedroom a TV-free zone? Keep a sleep diary and see how you feel – I bet you will notice a difference. You will find that you will read more too and that will send you off into a calm, deep sleep, which is so important for your general overall health.

Eat a reasonably good diet I am not about to tell you what that is. I think we all know by now that we all need to eat more vegetables. In fact, they should make up 40 per cent of your plate. Just lash them into you.

Practise JOMO I went to see Jerry Seinfeld a few years ago in the 3Arena and the opening part of the show was about how we all do the same thing when it comes to going out. We begin by talking about the fact that we are going out, how we are going to get there, where we will park, sit, who will be there, etc.; then we go out and straight away all we talk about is when we will leave and how much we are looking forward to getting home. It was so funny because it's true. I went out A LOT in my 20s and 30s. Pretty normal for most people that age, I think. But once I stopped drinking it made me sit back and ask myself what I really liked doing, and a big shocker to me was how much I loved just staying in and being at home. You can run yourself ragged accepting every invitation going but your main priority has to be you and your wellbeing. It's OK to say 'no thank you' to an invitation – you don't have to have a reason. I have zero FOMO. I practise JOMO – the joy of missing out – instead.

Have boundaries with people who create drama You know the type of person I'm talking about; there is always some sort of drama surrounding them and this person wants to drag you into it. It's hard to separate yourself from that, especially if you are the one whom this person usually vents to. But you have to set boundaries for your own mental health, and I swear you will feel so much better for it. Repeat after me: you do not have to involve yourself in other people's dramas.

Stop taking the little things (and yourself) too seriously Most things are not as big a deal as we make them out to be. You're running late for school – so what? You missed someone's birthday – they will be fine. You can't go to that party – it's grand, there will be other people there. You haven't called someone back – you can do it when you have the time, if you fancy. Once you start the process of easing up on this guilt, you will feel lighter and calmer. Try it.

Understand that this, too, shall pass Nothing stays the same, everything changes, good and bad. That means that when something is going really well, enjoy the experience, but at the same time, when something is going really bad, know that it will pass and things will get better. It's a lovely way to live your life as you can appreciate things in the here and now and know that life has a way of changing things, whether we like it or not.

Surround yourself with people who make you feel good This seems pretty obvious but you'd be amazed at the amount of people who spend time with people who make them feel bad about themselves. Do not give your precious time to others if they don't make you feel good about yourself. Life is way too short.

Remember that you will be dead forever The Stoic philosophers talk about something called a 'Memento Mori' – it's a way to remind yourself that you will die one day. Some people take this quite literally and place a picture of a skull beside their work desk; others tattoo it on their bodies. The idea is to continuously remind yourself that your time here on earth is finite so that you stop wasting your days worrying about shit that will probably never happen. Live your life in joy and recognise the fact that just being here is a miracle. Stop stressing and repeat 'I will be dead for ever' ad nauseam.

Be kind to yourself It's called self-compassion. I know, I know – it's hard to be nice to yourself, especially when you are last on your list. But it's really important to cut yourself some slack. You've heard it before, but you need to talk to yourself like your best friend would. I can be very harsh with myself. I expect a lot from myself and put myself under a lot of pressure. This is fine sometimes as we can all do with a kick up the arse every now and again, but if you are constantly being hard on yourself you need to stop and give yourself a break. I named my internal critical voice Jane. I think it's a great idea to name them because then you can stop the negative talk by telling your Jane to piss off. Remind yourself that you are doing your best and that is good enough.

STOP
STRESSING
AND REPEAT
'I WILL BE
DEAD
FOR EVER'
AD NAUSEAM.

Self-care: Beneficial, buzzword or big bucks?

 'I want some time out' sounds harsh.

'I need some me–time' sounds selfish.

'I'm practising some self–care' sounds softer, more acceptable, more marketable.

Taking care of yourself is what we are all supposed to do when we reach adulthood. The problem is that most women put themselves at the bottom of their 'care' list. So, they end up in a cycle of doing lots of self–*less* care while they mind everyone around them, from their partner to their kids to their ageing parents and colleagues.

As it stands, we're encouraged to have a good skin care routine, a fitness routine, a household routine, a routine around the routines and, ever since the wellness industry decided, we now must have a self–care routine too. If we were Taylor Swift, we'd be in our Never-ending, Plate–Spinning, Ball–Juggling era. It's EXHAUSTING.

The monetisation of self-care in recent years has bothered me. From luxury bath oils to pillow sprays for restful sleep, expensive journals, eye masks, scalp massagers, calming apps and whatever else you're having. Something that was so simple has become complicated and noisy and now it feels like self-care is yet another thing women HAVE to do.

And excuse me while I contradict myself here, but self-care *is* something that we all have to do, otherwise you (and I) will crack up. Nonetheless, some self-care routines that I've seen online are so unachievable that they make me feel that I'm failing even at this! You know the ones:

> *Wake at 5.30 a.m. and write in gratitude journal, followed by some soft body-brushing and then an outdoor ice bath, after that a cup of cacao and, finally, burn sage … Do all this before your commute from Portlaoise to Dublin.*

Self-care is about including YOU in the weekly plans, not just prioritising everyone else, so essentially, it's about time and choice. Time is something we cannot order online or buy by tapping our cards, and choice is free.

My self-care routine is like flying with Ryanair – no frills and full of rules

- Go to bed at a respectable hour instead of ploughing through yet another episode on Netflix/Paramount+/Disney+/Amazon Prime. I know I can watch it tomorrow.

- Avoid eating certain foods even though I really want them, because I know they hurt my tummy. (At 44 this has been the best self-care step I've ever taken. I love falafel but it doesn't love me.)

- I choose to go to the gym (instead of feeling like I have to).

- No thank you to caffeine after 3 p.m. (but I do love a decaf tea at night).

- I turn my phone to airplane mode when reading a book/ magazine or paper (how many times does your phone ping when you sit down to relax? Too many, I bet).

- I choose who I spend my free time with.

- I light a candle every evening (the family think I do it to get rid of those after-dinner smells from the air fryer, oven or pots and pans, but I do it just for me).

- I weed (not the illegal stuff). I get great pleasure from pulling weeds in my garden and I listen to podcasts at the same time.

- Now I'll contradict myself here for the second time and say I am partial to a good hair mask and face mask too the odd time (which are definitely not free ... hello, Space NK. I especially love a Patchology sheet mask).

Before PIN locks – there were real phone locks!

As a child of the '80s, there are two things I'm so grateful for:

- The music of Wham!
- Enjoying my entire childhood and adolescent years without a mobile phone.

While today's youth can obviously still enjoy the genius that was George Michael, they will never know what it's really like to disconnect. I'm sure most of you were like my family and had a landline in the hall, but ours had a lock on it. Yes, an actual lock that had to be opened with a key that was hidden by Mam. Only after permission had been granted could you swish the rotary dial by sticking your finger into the hole of the number and wheeling it in the correct sequence of digits.

If a boy said he'd phone me at seven o'clock, then I'd have to hang around the holy water font in our hall so I could jump on the phone after two, maybe three rings. And then there was the heart-thumping anxiety when the Telecom Éireann phone bill arrived, wondering if any sneaky calls I managed to make would now be found out.

But the parental control over the house phone meant I was always guarded, because my parents knew exactly who I was talking to and for how long. And if I didn't want to call someone, I had the very real excuse of 'Sorry, I wasn't allowed to use the phone.'

As I entered my early teens, I had a code with my friends that meant no phone charges. This secret scheme would involve ringing their landline three times and then hanging up. It had a different meaning each time: 'I'm finished my dinner' or 'I'm ready to walk to school' or 'I'm ready to go underage drinking'... basically each time it signalled 'I'm ready'.

Some fancy houses (like Jenny's) had more than one phone. While this indicated lottery-winning levels of wealth (remember that phone line rental was astronomical) it was also risky because it meant someone else could quite easily lift the handset in another room and listen in on your calls!

Passing a phone message on was as serious as taking the minutes of an AGM. We had an actual telephone message notepad and pen placed beside the locked phone so if any calls came in you HAD to write them down. God help me if I forgot to tell my mam that either of her sisters Ann or Sylvia had called for a chat.

Freedom!

At the age of 18 I got my first mobile phone, a Nokia 5110. It weighed about as much as a tin of beans but it doubled up as a fashion accessory because I could change the cover of the phone to match my clothes. I had three covers: light blue, red, and yellow. Instead of looking out the window I could now play Snake while on the number 40 bus going from Finglas to work in Arnotts. At first, I could only make calls, but then, without warning, Esat Digifone unlocked text messages for us pre-payers. *CU L8R!*

The sudden arrival of texts into my life was a game–changer. Making arrangements became so easy. I could be funnier, cheekier and even mildly sexier in my text messages, and the best part was I didn't have to hang around the hall of the house anymore – ever. The pure and almost innocent excitement of hearing the message notification ding and then seeing the tiny Nokia screen say:

$$\mathbf{!}$$

$$\mathtt{MESSAGE}$$

$$\mathtt{RECEIVED}$$

Because you didn't know who it was from until you clicked the 'read' button.

Step away from the phone …

Mobile phone etiquette

I copped on to having good mobile phone etiquette long before Roy Keane called out a journalist at *that* press conference. My mother was kind of like a female Roy. One Sunday afternoon I was texting while we were eating a roast dinner, and she banged the table so hard and shouted, 'GET OFF THAT STUPID THING!' I was completely lost in curating a perfect text and got such a fright that I dropped the phone (luckily those Nokia screens could withstand a bulldozer so it didn't smash). Maureen was right: it was and still is rude to be physically present but mentally elsewhere in a conversation with someone who is not at the table with you. The majority of our messages are not urgent and can wait until afterwards. She was ahead of her time.

Calls, texts and daily games of Snake on the bus — those were the good old phone days. Part of me wishes the technology had just stopped there.

‘ *We take better care of our smartphones than we do of ourselves*

— the phones are always recharged.

ARIANNA HUFFINGTON

How do I live without you?

The arrival of the smartphone has completely changed how we behave as a society. You only have to take your own head out of your phone and look around to see everyone else has their head down and eyes locked on their screen. We rely on it far too much — but the irony is that calling and actually talking is not the number one reason we use them. My phone feels like a necessity and often an addiction, too.

I once kept a note (on my phone, of course) of all the different reasons I picked up my phone over the course of a day:

- Turned off wake-up alarm
- Checked, read and sent emails
- Checked WhatsApp groups for kids' activities (Irish dancing)
- Sent a WhatsApp to a friend about a birthday celebration dinner (Lynda)
- Listened to a WhatsApp voice note that was 5 minutes and 43 seconds long
- Recorded and sent a voice note back to the same person that was 3 minutes and 27 seconds long
- Checked online banking
- Read a text from Bob in DHL regarding an impending delivery
- Bought a coffee and tapped my phone to pay
- Checked Instagram while in the loo
- Bought a top that I saw on Instagram (influenced by Jodie Wood)
- Used my camera to take yet another photo of my dog looking cute
- Paid for another after-school activity by Revolut

- Used the video camera at Bonnie's request to film her doing a handstand
- Listened to two podcasts
- Scrolled social media
- Read two articles from an Irish newspaper I've subscribed to
- Listened to the radio on a walk
- Looked for some inspiration for tonight's dinner
- Set my alarm for tomorrow

And ... I didn't 'phone' anyone.

We're on a scroll to nowhere

If scrolling is so bad, why does it feel so good? When my brain is bouncing all over the place with to-do lists and all the tasks not yet done and I really want to quieten down that noise, I scroll. Well, actually, I clean first (more of that later) but then when I need to just sit and be still, I'll scroll — and I love it. During these mindless scrolling sessions, I've discovered many a great new recipe to try, sorted out my fashion needs, found cleaning hacks, discovered interior trends and on more than one occasion I've had my entire mood lifted by watching a cute dog video. Sometimes I scroll for too long because I genuinely need to 'tap out' of all the things I have to do. And while this isn't a popular thing to say, when done in the right setting (THE TOILET), I find scrolling really relaxing. I know that makes me sound like a smoker from the 1950s.

But I've also experienced the opposite: reading a DM that's upset me, seeing a negative comment about me under a video, seeing other women manage to do incredible jobs and look like they're maintaining a good family life, too. Then I give myself a shake and remind myself that it's not real, it's all filtered and they are as flawed as I am.

Despite my love of scrolling, I monitor my own phone use around my daughters, who are just eight and six years old. Manners around smartphone use by parents will ultimately dictate how kids will use theirs when they eventually get one — monkey see, monkey do. And while we're on this, don't give your child a smartphone until they are in secondary school — they have no need for it before then.

The new rules

With phones and social media now so universal, it's time we all get some real boundaries around them. Here are my rules for regulating my phone use:

Lose the expectation that someone will reply immediately after you have texted them No one knows what the other person is doing at that moment, so just because it's been 'read' or the voice note has been listened to does not mean they are in a position to reply. And don't get into a snot with someone who hasn't replied for a day or two.

Just because you see someone is 'online' does not mean they are available (Or have the energy for chats or texts.)

Don't send nude photos – EVER! Only send photos that you would be happy to see in a frame.

Stick it on airplane mode, even when you're not flying You can still download and listen to your favourite podcast (*Jenny and Mairéad Now*, maybe?) but no one will interrupt you.

take flight ... mode, that is.

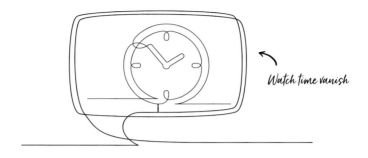

Watch time vanish

What the experts say

Outside of work, adults should have no more than two hours a day of screen time. But the average Irish person is spending more than three hours a day using their phone. Across the day, the mean time spent on a smartphone pick-up is around 1 minute 15 seconds. But if you're doing that 60 or 70 times a day, that is akin to putting vanishing cream on your time. We know smoking was the bad habit of previous generations – is this ours? The phone easily fits in our hand, we use it too often and we get a dopamine hit from it too. I wonder, in the not-too-distant future will there be ad campaigns telling us to quit?

ONLY SEND PHOTOS THAT YOU WOULD BE HAPPY TO SEE IN A FRAME.

(Un)Social media

J I have a real love/hate relationship with my phone. I am so glad that I grew up in a time when there was no social media. Everything can (some would say should) be chaotic in your 20s. You are finding out who you are and what you like (and don't like), so it's all about experimentation, and with that comes some mad times. And the expression 'what goes on tour stays on tour' exists for a reason. If you are wondering what I did on these weekends and nights out ... thankfully, they are lost to memory. And we didn't have mobile phones to film any of it, so it's like it never happened.

Communicating but not connecting

Mobile phones and social media were heralded as life-enhancing inventions that would keep us all connected, and yet young people are sadder, lonelier and more disconnected than ever. We are communicating with so many people through our phones but not actually connecting in real life. It's such a new technology that there is little research into the long-term consequences of social media use, but there have been some studies that have found the more time spent on social media, the more social anxiety, depression and loneliness we experience. It IS affecting our mental health, but because it is proven to be addictive it is almost impossible to put down once the scrolling begins. We like and want that dopamine hit. And we are giving these things to our young children! I am not anti-technology, but I feel deeply saddened when walking back from dropping my kids to school and I see young students walking with their heads down, staring at their phones, ignoring the world and those around them before heading into school for the day. It reminds me of shuffling zombies.

And that's why I've thrown my phone away.

OK, no, I haven't.

Why not? Because it is almost impossible to live without it nowadays. I have two kids and I'm essentially their secretary, which means I'm in endless WhatsApp groups – the bloody bane of my life. If I were not in these groups, I would miss out on too many things in their lives.

I have a dream ...

To live in a world without a mobile phone. Maybe when my kids are older, I'll start slowly removing myself from the tyranny of my phone. I will switch to a Nokia. Text only. I feel this would make my life better and more productive. There are mobile-free coffee shops popping up here and there, places that push for real social interaction – you know, talking to each other.

So, it is pretty obvious that we need rules for how we (and our children) use phones. We need to help ourselves. There has to be basic social media etiquette – I know what my personal rules are:

- No phones at the table when food is being served.
- No playing loud 'funny' videos without headphones in.
- No talking loudly on public transport or in coffee shops about your fungal nail infection on your big toe or your sister's piles being 'like a bunch of grapes' after her third child.

A friend of mine once said these immortal words that I *try* to live by – 'My phone is for my convenience, not yours.' WOW!

What we know now about

death & grief

OR, WHY EVERYONE SAYS STUPID THINGS AT FUNERALS

You don't stop loving

M You don't stop loving the people you love after they die, even though you can't ever see, hear or hold them again. Even though all that's left are their possessions and your memories with them. When I think of my mother, and I often do, I remember her being SO affectionate and having the best pair of legs I've ever seen. She spoiled me with attention and affection because I was a big 'surprise' to her at 40.

At the very young age of 58, Mam was diagnosed with breast cancer and subsequently had a mastectomy and nine months of chemo. In the days after her 60th birthday party she was back in hospital for another surgery because the cancer had raised its ugly head again. Radiation this time, every day for six weeks. That finished in late September and then in early December that year Mam had severe back pain. It's the only time I remember her calling in sick to work (she loved her job as a waitress in Clontarf Castle).

On 21 December she went to hospital to get results from a recent scan and the news was awful. The oncologist told Mam that her cancer was terminal and she had possibly nine months left, at most. The offer of more treatments was made, but my brave mam declined. She had peacefully accepted what lay ahead.

What I know now

Life will carry on as normal while your world is falling apart
It was Christmas week. At times like this you realise that all the shopping and gift-wrapping is nonsense because the one thing we wanted for Christmas was for all of this to go away. But the disease wasn't going anywhere. Mam was admitted to hospital immediately, which meant all of Christmas was spent in the Mater. I visited her there on New Year's Eve night just to show her my new one-shoulder dress I had bought in River Island. Then off I went to McGowans in Phibsboro and got really drunk.

She came home sometime in January, but that's all a bit of a blur because life goes on as normal and everyone had returned to work. All the while, we knew our mother was dying ... slowly, but quickly too.

Mam's last night out was to celebrate my sister Olga's 30th birthday at the end of January. She was in a huge amount of discomfort that night but refused to miss it, because Olga (the middle child) was always her favourite. She was the daughter who made her laugh like no one else could.

During Mam's short illness I got to see and understand the unique relationships we all had with her. Even though we were adults I knew she was worried about us in different ways. The irony is that Mam thought I was shy and quiet and was concerned that people might take advantage of me. Which is funny, because I can be as tough as a well-done steak when I need to be.

She would never have thought that I'd end up with a career in media. She saw none of it, but that side of things wouldn't have mattered to her. All she ever wanted for her three girls was for us to be happy.

Unfortunately, our lovely mam Maureen didn't get to see some of the happiest times in our lives because she died on 2 April 2001 in St Francis' Hospice in Raheny. It was the night before my 21st birthday.

Familiarity and routine things will save you in times when your idea of normal is rapidly disintegrating A few hours after Mam's death, I went home and got stuck into cleaning the house because she was coming home the next day to be laid out. She had always been house-proud so I wanted to make sure the place was sparkling for her final nights at home. I felt like it was the final thing I could do for her. Writing this down, I realise how silly that sounds – she was dead and couldn't see the hours of cleaning I'd done. I should have just sat still, drunk tea and eaten chocolate instead. But while my mam's death was the end of her, it was the beginning of something else, something all of us will experience but none of us are prepared for – grief.

Everyone will say stupid things because they don't know what to say (including yourself!) I said some very gobshite-y things often around the time of my mam's funeral, like, 'Well at least she's not in pain anymore,' and 'At least she died looking like herself' and that old classic, 'She's at peace now.' In those moments, I genuinely believed the ridiculous things coming out of my own mouth. That's

Gobshite-y

why I'm a lot more forgiving of the clichéd things people say around a death.

My much older sisters took me and my then-boyfriend out for dinner on the night of my 21st birthday, the same day Mam's body was laid out at home. A bizarre thing for all of us to do, but they felt that she would have wanted them to do that. There's a lot of that talk after a death – 'It's what he/she would have wanted'– when actually, unless the dead person stated it beforehand, none of us have a clue what they wanted. So, instead of dressing it up as something else, just say, 'Here's what I want to do – get out of the house for a few hours and have someone hand me dinner and some drinks.'

Dad stayed home with Mam while we were gone. When we got home, tipsy from wine and tired from five nights in the hospice and crying – crying is exhausting – we played her favourite music, which was the soundtrack to *Out of Africa* (Mam never visited Africa, she just loved the film and soundtrack), a bit of Barry Manilow because his song 'Even Now' was her party piece, and Westlife (yes, Westlife are on the go that long!).

But the surprising thing is that during those first few days I was fine. I was sad, I did cry lots, but I was fine.

You will get through the funeral more easily than you think

The funeral was overwhelming, so many people to talk to, so many hands to shake and so many stories to listen to. But a bit like Queen Elizabeth, Maureen had planned everything. I suppose you can do that when you're told that death is imminent. She chose the hotel for lunch, the food and the music. As funerals go, it was a good one; had she been a mourner at her own funeral she would have complimented everything from the mass ('lovely mass') to the music ('beautiful choir') to the flowers ('the flower arrangements were magnificent') and her daughters ('those three girls looked very elegant').

It's the little things that will cause the most pain in the aftermath – like no light in the porch There are some days of Mam's illness that have vanished from my memory, but there is one that even now, after 23 years, still stings when I remember it: arriving home the night of Mam's funeral. It was as though our home was telling us that she was really gone. The house was in total darkness; no porch light, no soft lamps on in the living room, no radio on (which acted as a security alarm before we had one – Mam always said that if someone broke in, they'd hear voices and leave without taking a thing). The house was suddenly different, and it's never been the same since. What makes a house a home? It's the people living in it. Mam was the heartbeat of Number 84; without her, it was just a three-bed, detached house with a decently sized garage.

Everyone grieves in their own way – don't judge them I spent the next few months partying, going out to everything and generally having a great time. I was 21 with no mother to tell me what to do (yes, I had my dad, but the boss was dead and he was not going to try to take her place now). When friends, neighbours or family tried to ask, 'How are you?' I would reiterate the stupid funeral clichés: 'I'm OK, because Mam was really sick, so it's better she's at peace now, she's not in pain anymore.' And then on to the next night out. Quite often I saw my sister Olga crying so hard that she almost couldn't breathe, and I thought, 'Pull yourself together! This wasn't a shock; we KNEW Mam was dying!'

My life as one big party continued. I started studying media in college five months after her death. To me, college was BRILLIANT; it was like *Love Island* but we wore polo necks and didn't have a pool. I thrived there. A year later, I managed to get work experience in Today FM and that was also ONE HUGE PARTY.

What I know now is that, during this time, I was experiencing suppressed or delayed grief. I showed no real outward signs of grief, nothing like my dad or my sisters who were causing floods with the amount of tears they cried. But my grief was affecting me physically. For the entire year of 2001 I was ill every month; a tummy bug, a severe throat infection, my first ever kidney infection, another tummy bug, a second kidney infection, an ear infection and another throat infection, which eventually lead to a trip to Beaumont Hospital for tonsil removal – at 21! AND my hair started to go grey.

Grief was literally coming out of my pores. And still I kept pushing it down, squishing it into the pit of my now very delicate stomach (I also became a puker). In a way, it was like wearing Spanx … when your dress is on it all looks great on the outside, but underneath, the bits have to go somewhere.

In one of the last conversations I had with Mam, she told me she wanted to grab the cancer in her body and wring its neck. But, unable to do that, she accepted her fate and told me, 'I can do far more for you up there than I ever can down here.' So, every opportunity that came my way, I took it as a sign that my mam was pulling strings 'up there'. Every nice thing that happened to me, every college assignment that went well, every job opportunity or new person that came into my life, I thought – 'Is Mam doing this?'

You can be happy and sad at the same time But my delayed grief hit hard six years – yes, SIX years – after her death. When I had my first child, my beautiful boy Dara, it was one of the happiest times of my life. But it made me realise how much my mam had loved me, and I was so sad that I was only realising this now. I cried a lot while feeding and just generally staring at this gorgeous baby who was mine, telling him, 'Nana Maureen would have adored you so much.' I had finished playing whack-a-mole with my feelings. I let the heartache ache. I let my thoughts go to places where I hadn't allowed them and let the tears come back – this time because I actually felt the loss, the robbery, the unfairness.

I became jealous of friends who still had their mams.

I let anger arrive — anger with everyone, even Mam. Did Mam let the lump get too big before acting? Did her doctors miss something?

I let disappointment surface.

And eventually, I let go.

I let go of all the talk of what might have been: the shopping trips that never happened, the hotel getaway we never got to go on, the advice I didn't get from her, the what-ifs, the memories not made, because my life now had to go on and I had to exist without her.

Grief is part of me. I live with it every day. But time (lots of it), talking (lots of it) and therapy (you'll know yourself) have helped me to survive it.

YOU CAN BE HAPPY AND SAD AT THE SAME TIME.

Sudden death

J Thursday night, 7 April 2011. I was getting myself sorted for the next day's work. We were late back from an outside broadcast in Mullingar when my phone rang. It was my dad. Originally from Westmeath, he wanted to hear all about the day and who I had met. He was heading off to the races in Aintree the next morning. I told him he would not have as good a time as last year, when we were all there together as a family. He said, 'Sure, we'll do it again next year.' The call ended with his usual 'Bye, bye, bye'.

The next morning, while on air on Today FM, I spotted my boss outside the studio waving for me to come out. When the ad break came on, I stood up and walked out to him, jokingly saying, 'Ohhh, am I in trouble?' He brought me into his office and told me that my 66-year-old dad, Michael, had died suddenly during the night.

Here's what the worst of times has taught me

Sudden death is very difficult to accept and understand My brain did not want to believe the incomprehensible truth that my dad was dead. It seemed impossible that his life force was gone. Where was he? How could he just disappear? I felt as if I was standing behind a glass partition, cut off from everyone, acting out my normal life. Looking back, I see that this was my way of coping with something too huge and too shocking to comprehend.

Grief will show you how resilient you are I thought death equalled drama, tears and beating of chests. But I found it to be a lot quieter than that. A low-level dread, waves of emotion that never fully took me over, that I somehow managed to manage – usually by pushing the feelings down and down and down. And that works, until it doesn't. It is true what they say, it has to come out somehow, but in my case, it was more like a leaking tap than a tsunami of grief. I felt if I had let the full magnitude of my feelings wash over me back then, I could have drowned and possibly would not have recovered from it.

But guess what? Even after all these years of managing it and pushing the feelings down, I have not recovered from it. Because the truth is, you are not supposed to recover from it. You have to be it, absorb it, feel it. I wear my dad's death around me like a blanket. I keep myself tightly wrapped up in it, cosy and warm. Others may feel that they desperately need to get it out of them or away from them. I can understand that too. We each have to do what is best for us, but it is a step-by-step process, and as difficult as that is to hear when it first happens to you, it is the truth. Grief is a very lonely thing. It is a sadness that you never fully shake but that you learn to live with.

When someone you love dies, you will instantly join a club of bereaved people You will recognise them immediately, as they will sweep you up into their arms, fully acknowledging your pain because they recognise it. The others around you who have not yet experienced this grief will do their best, but it's almost impossible for them to know what you are going through.

People will disappear from your life because they are unable to be around your grief It may frighten them or make them feel uncomfortable. Either way, you have to understand that this is all about them and not you.

Bringing or sending food is one of the most helpful things you can do for someone who is grieving I remember a family friend organising the food for my dad's wake. It was such a caring thing to do when the whole family was in such shock. And in the days after the funeral, neighbours arrived with dinners, all made with care and love. It was their way of expressing their condolences to our whole family.

A handwritten card expressing sympathy means so much to a grieving person I still have all the emails that were sent into Today FM from our wonderful listeners telling me how sorry they were to hear about my dad's sudden death. They had heard me talk about him on air and could sense my love and understand my huge loss. I was overwhelmed by their kindness.

Humour can be found even in the saddest moments My sister Suzanne and I had to choose the coffin for our dad. Sitting in the 'good' family room and flicking through a folder full of pictures of coffins made us laugh uncontrollably. People looked on, thinking we had lost our minds.

And on the night before the funeral, my cousin Niamh and I were desperately trying to write the prayers of the faithful, when we noticed my dad's coffin lid with his name on it beside us. The surreal awfulness of the situation made us laugh hysterically till we cried.

Just sitting with someone who is grieving and drinking tea with them is as good as any advice In fact, don't give advice; just sit there and be with them. Let a grieving person talk about their pain and the person they are missing. It is not your job to cheer them up, and trying to do this will make them not want to open up to you. And remember, a grieving person won't always want to talk, so don't push them. Suggest a walk in nature instead. Remember that the months after someone dies can be the loneliest time for a bereaved person, so just being there can be all they need.

Grief never ends but that is the beauty of it. Love never ends.

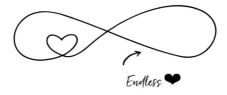

Endless ♥

What we know now about ↘

careers

OR, WHY YOU CAN'T HAVE IT ALL

A DULL one or a WOW one?

J I've found that most people are not impressed if you tell them that you are a stay-at-home mum. It's as if a large sign saying DULL appears above my head. I've learned to internally laugh when it happens — probably because I've had it both ways: the DULL reaction and the WOW one. OK, maybe not WOW, but definitely a more interested reaction.

When I made the decision to step back from my work in radio in 2014, I got to hear a lot of people's opinions. Most of them were not positive. It was difficult for others to understand how I could just 'give up' my career after I had spent so long getting to where I was. Some female listeners felt that it was anti-feminist, that by turning my back on my working life and returning to the drudgery of the kitchen sink I was setting a bad example to others. But at this stage I had two children, aged eight and two, and the sudden death of my beloved dad in 2011 had made me stop and reassess my life and consider what was really important to me. And yes, I loved my career, but I was finding it more and more difficult to leave my children every day, especially knowing that this time with them would go by in the blink of an eye. I did not want to be lying on my deathbed thinking that I had missed out on being there with them during their childhoods. I wanted that, and I was incredibly lucky to even have that choice.

This is a very emotive subject. All I can say is that I am talking about my own thought process in deciding to stop working to be at home with my children. There is no judgement on any other woman's life choice. How could there be? You don't know my full situation and I don't know yours.

When a big decision has to be made, quieten down and block out all the external noise.

That's what I did and once my decision was made, it was easy. I really did not care what others thought because I knew that I was making the right decision for me and for our family.

So, in June 2014 I stepped back from work as a radio producer/presenter and became a stay-at-home mum. Though I actually hate that name – it is so patronising. I prefer to think of myself as a mother who minded her children full time. Actually, that might be worse …

'You might be having a heart attack'

I was at home for around six months when Ray made the move to the afternoon show on RTÉ Radio 1 along with a Saturday night chat show. After lots of talking, we decided that I would go back as one of the producers on the radio show. Setting up a new radio show takes time and consistency, so the reasoning was that I would be able to help 'bed it in'. It was not ideal but it was always a short-term plan (in my head, anyway). So, I went back to work in January 2015 in RTÉ. At the same time, I decided to get a new Golden Retriever puppy and threw training for a marathon into the mix as well. A psychologist would have something to say about that.

It all came to a head in June 2015, when I ended up in the Black-rock Clinic, doing a stress test for chest pains. When I went to my GP and described my symptoms, a tight band of pain around my upper torso, he told me they were classic heart attack symptoms in women and sent me straight down to have it checked out. It seemed ridiculous to me; I was super fit after running the marathon in April and ended up doing the stress test on a fully inclined treadmill, not even out of breath. Guess what? It was all stress related. I had never in my life thought of myself as a stressed person, but here I was. I knew that something had to change. Here was my body giving me a massive sign to take notice of, and at the same time I felt that no one was steering the ship at home and that work was once again taking over everything. I knew I had to return to my original decision to be at home with the children, so a plan was put in place and I left my working life once again in 2016.

You CAN'T have it all

One of the best decisions I've ever made was deciding to be at home with my two children, but to be completely honest there were times when I felt like I was losing myself a little. My career had given me purpose and meaning and I felt some days that all I had achieved was a series of menial, thankless jobs — make the beds, clean up breakfast, wash down the sinks, clean the loos, sweep the floors, quick *tsss, tsss* of the spray mop, fold the throws on the couch, fluff up the cushions on the couch, fold the clothes from the dryer, put the folded clothes away, put on a wash … and it's not even 10 a.m.

I had this nagging voice in my head telling me that I was letting myself down by not achieving more. But I didn't know if I could trust that voice — was it just my ego? I was very happy, leading a very calm life, so I was confused about why there was a part of me that felt drawn back to a busier, more ego-driven life.

Heart over head

Up to that point in 2016, I believed in absolutes. I thought any decision I made should be based on detached pragmatism and that I should be certain that it was the right one. That was not the case here. My decision was based on my emotions and knowing that this was what I needed to do. And because of that, it has made me reassess what I thought to be true for most of my adult life.

Allow your priorities to change with you

I was under the impression that your career should be nearly every-thing to you, that ambition and focus were solid, strong character traits and that what you did for work said so much about you. But now, I don't really feel that way. My career is just one part of my life. But I won't lie, it was difficult to unlearn all these strongly held core beliefs. The 'you should be doing more' voice in my head was loud at times.

Get talking!
(If that's your thing)

Find creative satisfaction outside your job

A strange thing had happened in the few short years I had been out of the workplace: I lost confidence in my abilities. Where before I would have just given something a go, now I was stuck in a tailspin of doubt-ing what I was capable of and feeling a bit at sea. I had spoken to Ray about how I was feeling and realised I was missing creativity. I had to consider the things that made me happy outside of looking after everyone at home and nurture my creative side. Ray basically pushed me into our home studio, stuck a microphone in my face and said, 'TALK'. We started doing a podcast together and it felt great. Ray and I had met through work and spent all our 'getting to know each other' years in the studio together, so this was a place that felt so easy to me. I feel more myself 'on air' or with a microphone in front of me than anywhere else. We loved doing our podcast together but then the seed was planted for me to branch off into another podcast. I needed my other partner in crime for this ... enter Mairéad Ronan.

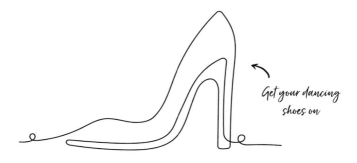

Get your dancing shoes on

Working your gut

M I've always been a big believer in that old chestnut, 'Trust your gut.' You know when something seems like a mad idea and everyone is saying, 'No, no, no, don't do that,' but that feeling in the pit of your stomach is saying, 'It's OK to do it. Trust me.' It's steered me in the right direction over the years, and at times I've ignored a strong belly feeling and regretted it later.

When my third child was about seven weeks old, I got a call from a production company called Shinawil, asking if I would be interested in taking part in their new series of *Dancing with the Stars*. My fitness was on the floor and my breasts were enormous from feeding – not a great combination for dancing on the telly! But I was a huge fan of the show and my gut was telling me to give it a go. I said yes and got to work almost immediately trying to piece myself back together again. Family and friends were concerned – I had this tiny baby, a 2-year-old, an 11-year-old and a house extension and renovation going on. But ...

I've been conditioned to think that work is the most important thing in life. Get up, get out there and get on with things even if you're a little under the weather (or you've just had a baby). Part of that is because of how my parents viewed work, but it also comes from being in the media. You take all the gigs you can, because each one might be your last. In a way, you're always on shaky ground, so I've needed that gut reaction to steady things.

How was I going to get through all of this? Easy, by working my unfit arse off. Expressing milk for Bonnie during rehearsals, feeding her at night, choosing taps and tiles while learning the tango too. The night I did my first live dance, Bonnie turned 5 months. I was in full-on Dory mode: 'Just keep swimming (or dancing).'

Fast forward 12 weeks (which included a great Charleston, a decent contemporary ballroom, a terrible jive and a perfect-scoring Viennese waltz), I won the series. I'd had the time of my life (pardon the dance reference) but I was WRECKED.

Back to the day job ... again

Winning *DWTS* brought lots of offers of work, including the chance to present a daily radio show on Today FM. This was something I'd ALWAYS wanted. So, my gut and ego agreed. I felt really comfortable going back to Today FM because to me she has always been like another family (cheesy but true). I started working there before I had finished college, making tea and posting prizes, and now I had my name over the door at lunchtime each day. I had a great producer and I loved having the chats with listeners and being part of their daily routine. I was back in my busy, busy bee zone. Busy is where I always felt I belonged.

What do you WANT to do with your life?

Then Covid hit. I went from working in a noisy, bustling, energetic office to an empty, soulless space. My producer Pam was sent to work from home and could only communicate with me during the show by typing on screen.

Like most people at that time, I had to do my job each day and do it to the same standard as usual but without any of the support systems I had put in place — one of those being childcare. The pandemic really changed me — it changed how I view my world, how I value my time, my friendships and how I want to live the next (hopefully) 45 years of my life. I had never really thought about that before, because when you're always busy you don't have time to think. What do I want to do? Where do I want to be? Am I having a midlife crisis? I also realised the majority of the stuff I worried about was work-related and, ultimately, unimportant. When I was really honest with myself I knew what I wanted and where I wanted to be: it was at home spending more time with my loves.

The beginning of the end

(or, inside the mind of a stressed-out working mother)

I began having conversations with Louis about leaving my 'dream job' to be home with the kids full-time. Louis listened but each time gave me the same line: 'No one can make this decision for you.'

So I WRECKED my head every day for months with thoughts like:

- 'I want to be with the children all the time.'
- 'The kids will drive me mad and I will miss working so much.'
- 'They grow up so fast – look at Dara, he's a man child now towering over me at 14 (his age at the time).'
- 'The kids will eat better food if I'm home more.'
- 'The kids do love a Goodfellas pizza, so that really won't change.'
- 'I'll lose my independence – I've always had my own money.'
- 'I'll see my dad more if I'm not so busy.'
- 'I love my job, and the listeners.'
- 'I'll return to radio when the girls are older – and that will fly by.'
- 'I'll never get any job in media again.'
- 'I have such a laugh in work.'
- 'If I leave I'm letting so many people down.'
- 'But I want to get off this very fast treadmill.'
- 'I'll still work, doing other things, at my own pace.'
- 'What if no work is offered to me ever again?'

But I kept coming back to: I want to be at home with the kids more.

My brain felt like a piece of Play-Doh, getting mauled everyday with all these different thoughts. I couldn't actually make a decision with my head ... so I made it with my heart and the old reliable gut.

What's right ... right now?

A meeting was arranged with my radio boss about signing a new contract. I arrived, ready with my speech, which I'd practised the night before with Louis. I took a deep breath, started talking and didn't stop. It was a mini-rant, albeit a professional one. I explained that I couldn't sign another contract because I wanted to be at home with the kids. 'They are growing too fast and I feel like I don't see them and I'm so tired from juggling home and work all the time and I just want to be there ... And, and, and, and ...' and I eventually stopped talking.

James (the boss man) was genuinely shocked. He sat back in his chair, folded his arms and was quiet for a moment. Then he said, 'My daughter has just got her place in university, and I can't believe she's at that stage of her life, so I get it, I understand.' I was so relieved – relieved that he (being a man) didn't think that I was a loon or a let-down. We agreed that I would stay on for another 6 months and could then say goodbye on-air. On my last day there I knew I had made the correct decision. I was going to be exactly where I wanted to be right at that moment ... home.

There is no perfect – every decision comes with some sacrifices

Of course, there are the odd days that I miss the buzz of being live on air, chatting and laughing with listeners and being around lovely work colleagues. But I don't miss it enough to give up what I have right now and that is a solid gut feeling: I am exactly where I want to be. My head knows it, my heart feels it and my gut agrees with them both.

Women now have to earn bread and then serve bread, too

My mother always worked, but it was part-time and I knew it was something she really enjoyed too. But even then, it was a choice for her; she didn't have to work, because my dad's salary was enough. But for the majority of families, that choice has been taken away. I know I'm in a privileged position to *have* been able to decide to step away from work for a time.

It would be wonderful if we could all do exactly what we want in this situation: work lots, work less, work part-time, work just when the kids are in school, take a career break ... but unfortunately, the first thing that needs to be looked at is finances. With rising living costs, inflation, creche and childminding fees ... sometimes no matter how you do the maths, the answer is *damned if you do (work), damned if you don't.*

Will the sacrifice of giving up my job give me back something else?

Well ... you immediately become the CEO (of home) so that's already a promotion. You will also be a personal assistant, secretary, taxi driver, chef, household manager, personal shopper, concierge, dog walker, cleaner, clown, entertainer and head of law enforcement. But for me, it's all been worth it because I gave myself the gift of time.

Things to bear in mind if you're thinking about it too

- Remember, it's not about giving up on your ambitions, it's about giving yourself what you need right now and trusting yourself to know that.

- When the time is right, work will come again.

- Make an effort to keep your network alive by staying in touch with work colleagues: there may be some contract work or holiday cover that might suit your needs in the short term.

- Value the skills you learn at home – I have become a far more patient person (not just with the kids but with annoying adults, too).

- Do the maths on the savings made by stepping back. This involves doing a deep dive on the costs of childcare, after-school activities, commuting and the 'invisible cloak' expenses, such as coffees. (You don't see them, but they are there.)

- Realistically, we know you either need a partner's income supporting the family or six months of your salary saved to be able to take a step back.

- Talk to a career coach – because each situation is unique.

THERE IS NO PERFECT — EVERY DECISION COMES WITH SOME SACRIFICES.

What we know now about

self-acceptance & getting older

OR, WHY IT'S GREAT TO NOT BE A SPRING CHICKEN

The narrative around ageing seems to be how terrible it all is — our bodies failing us, our minds slowing down, our looks fading, our voices no longer heard. Well, we think we need to flip that narrative on its head. We're programmed to believe that getting older is something to dread and fear. Sure, the realisation that we are not here for ever now firmly stares us in the face, but so too does the knowledge that, if you are lucky enough to have your health, getting older can be a very freeing and interesting time. It's a time for self-reflection, allowing you to think about what you want to do with the rest of your fabulous life.

Thin, in between, up and down and up again

J From around the age of nine, I began to put on weight. It was quite unusual back in the 1980s. Was it my genes or my trips to Paula's sweet shop or my love of mayonnaise sandwiches that piled on the weight? I'm not sure. I was a very active child and loved being outdoors and playing sports in school. Who knows why some of us struggle with our weight and others don't? I've read and watched programmes on the whys and all I know is since the time I first began to put on weight it's been part of my life. The up and down of it all.

When I was in second year in school, a boy in the year above made a comment on my weight. I realised pretty quickly that in order to fit in and be acceptable, I had to make myself smaller. So, I cut back on food and became thin. I was not happier, and it didn't seem to make a lot of difference to anyone.

I went to college in the Samuel Beckett Centre in Trinity College (now called The Lir Academy) and I have college reports from the end of term specifically telling me to 'lose the weight' and that I was 'not a fat person'. I was a size 12.

I'd like to think that things have changed for younger women nowadays but I don't think they have; if anything, it's worse. There's more pressure and more bullshit to look at and to compare yourself to. And yet we are told to be 'body confident whatever your size'. It's a lot more complicated than that for women. The idea of body confidence is confusing to me, because I don't feel confident when I am big. I feel shame. I remember being fitted for my school uniform and the woman in the shop saying to my mum, 'Oh, she's a big fine girl.' And I felt shame. I remember when I ran the Paris Marathon, a female colleague congratulated me and then said, 'It's great to see someone like you, you know, not a Skinny Minnie, doing it.' And I felt shame. I remember a man sidling up to me on an outside broadcast and whispering in my ear, 'I didn't think you'd be big.' And I felt shame.

Shame feels like a whole-body, burning sensation.

We have been programmed to believe that our worth lies in how attractive the world perceives us to be. And the world tells us that attractive means thin (but with boobs and a bum).

But, very slowly, for me it has become more about health than looks, and with that comes an easing-up of the perceived outside pressure on what I should look like. Now, it's more about what feels right for me physically.

And I am very grateful to my body for carrying me around for the last 50-odd years. I make a point of thanking my body after a good weights or yoga session or a run. I thank it for its strength and for its health. It's a wonderful body that has brought my two children into the world, has allowed me to run a marathon, go trekking up mountains in Nepal, walk my gorgeous dogs and dive into the sea. It's a body that is strong and healthy, so for all that I am very grateful. That is the first time I have ever written down a thanks to my body, and it feels quite good. Maybe try it the next time you find you are thinking negative thoughts about yourself.

SHAME
FEELS
LIKE A
WHOLE-BODY,
BURNING
SENSATION.

My body ...
I've been an awful bitch to her

M I had a cup of tea in hand as I read Jenny's piece, and I cried. I too have experienced so many incidents which made me feel shame about my body. But surely the real problem is that every single one of us has been unhappy with our size, shape or weight. Why do we allow ourselves to speak so negatively about our bodies when we know it is the only place we have to live?

My body has been a really good friend to me, but I've been a bitch to her. She's always been there working away; heart pumping, lungs breathing, kidneys filtering, liver cleansing, bowels moving and brain active (albeit a little forgetful these days). Despite this, I've been a terrible friend to her.

Too often I've spoken badly about her. Too often I've criticised her when she didn't deserve it. Too often I've wished she looked different – smaller waist, longer legs, more hair on my head, less hair elsewhere.

I don't want to say anything that may make my mother sound unkind, because she was so loving, caring and affectionate. But she, like so many women of her time, was extremely body–conscious. One example of this was on the morning of my 18th birthday. After she had given me my gifts and a big birthday hug, she also gave me some advice: 'Mairéad, now that you're eighteen, you need to curb that big appetite.' It was one of those moments where a comment intended to be helpful was actually hurtful.

I've lost count over the years of the times when complete strangers have said to me, 'You're a lot smaller than I thought', or 'You look much bigger on the telly.' Those good aul' back–handed compliments that are actually are thinly veiled insults. Women are hard enough on themselves about their bodies without anyone else's input.

Jenny often uses a quote from author Sophie Lark: *'Your looks are the least interesting thing about you.'* I really believe that with all my heart, but if anyone can figure out a way to bottle that sentiment so I can actually live it every day of my life, please let me know and I'll buy a crate.

With ageing comes acceptance or, as we say, a large dose of COP ON. I am now less of a bitch and far kinder to my body than I've ever been. Because I've finally realised that, apart from dodgy tonsils and a thyroid gland that's not up to much, my body has got me to 44 years of age illness-free. It has cooked and delivered to me three beautiful, healthy children. It has run three half-marathons and completed one adventure race. It has even won a dance competition on live television – what more do I want from her?

Well, since you asked, I want her to keep going for decades more. I want her to keep working all the bits exactly like she has. Because, honestly, I feel like I'm just getting started.

I was born to be middle-aged

J **I've never felt more content or freer than I do now that I am in my 50s. I think there was a part of me that was always waiting for this bit.**

- I like that I never eat dinner later than 7.30 p.m. (dinner at 9 p.m. may as well be midnight).
- I like being in nature as opposed to clubs.
- I like seeing friends one on one, rather than in big groups.
- I like going to the movies rather than the pub.
- I love putting on my pyjamas and making a cup of tea before settling in to watch Netflix.
- I love going to bed early with my book.

I was a bit at sea in my 20s and some of my 30s. I thought that I was here to figure the world out and my place in it rather than understanding that all the while I was just getting to know myself. The older I get, the more comfortable I become in my own skin.

Studies have shown that our overall levels of happiness are at their lowest in our 30s and 40s when we are right smack-bang in the middle of young kids, ageing parents, job stresses and financial worries. After the age of 50, we start slowly but surely getting happier. Some studies explain this ageing happiness phenomenon by saying that the older you get, the more you choose to be happy. You make a conscious decision to surround yourself with relationships that are satisfying, begin to focus on what feels good rather than working towards things you are told you should have, and you become less self-conscious and self-critical.

Here are some things to love about getting older

- You worry less about other people's opinions.

- You understand that you have two ears and one mouth for a reason.

- You know what you like and don't like and you don't waste time doing the things you don't like.

- You appreciate your internal health more than your appearance. That's not to say that you stop caring about how you look, but it becomes a little bit less important.

- You know who you like to spend time with.

- You don't put up with bad attitudes or negative vibes.

- You understand that vulnerability is what it means to be human.

- You know that time is finite and you cherish the time you do have.

- You are more patient with yourself and others.

- You understand that 'having it all' means something completely different now to what you thought it meant in your 20s.

- You try not to take yourself (or anyone else) too seriously.

- You feel less sure about things. This is freeing as opposed to frightening. You see that most things are multilayered and complicated and not simply black or white.

Getting older can be the most freeing and interesting time in your life

Introspection gets a bad rep. It's seen as being a bit up yourself, a bit self-absorbed. But I'd argue that not enough of us are taking the time to get to know ourselves and ask ourselves who we really are. Introspection is a necessary part of ageing and will hopefully get you to a point where you do know yourself so much better – and then comes the freedom part.

Not paying attention to what others think allows you to just please yourself without worrying about people's perception of you. Seems impossible? Then you are definitely a good candidate.

Try saying no a little bit more. Add in a few 'I'll see how I feel's and mix in the odd, 'That's not my kind of thing but thanks for the invite's and *WOW* – your mind will explode.

It's kind of exciting and feels a bit bold, but after a while it becomes easy and one day you are just living your life, saying yes to things you want to do and no to things you don't.

How simple. Now that's freedom.

But be prepared for the kickback from those who are not used to you saying no. You might get told you're selfish or you've changed. Think of these as positive responses rather than criticisms – you are now well on your way to ageing well.

Your looks are the least interesting thing about you

I have this weird thing – maybe you have it too – but after I get to know someone, I stop seeing their face. I mean, of course they still have a face, but what I get when I am around them is more of a feeling, a

warmth and a glow – some might say an aura. It means that how someone looks is so much less important to me than how they make me feel. And I think that is how we humans all eventually see each other. How long can we stare at someone who is irresistibly good-looking, admiring their beauty? Eventually that becomes irrelevant, and it's how they make you feel that shines through. Roald Dahl had it right when he wrote, 'If you have good thoughts, they will shine out of your face like sunbeams and you will always look lovely.'

But you look a little sad

I've thought about giving myself a helping hand, a freshener–upper, a more 'rested' look. I've looked into that mirror and seen the deep 11s between my eyes and the tear–trough eye bags that do not disappear and make me look tired even after I've had lots of sleep. I've played around with the filter on Instagram and seen how I could look 10 years younger … but at the end of the day I'm doing all my viewing from my eyes. I'm not looking at myself all the time, so I can ignore it *most* of the time. That sounds like such a mammy thing to say – 'Stop looking at yourself' – but it's true. Maybe if we stopped looking in mirrors and examining our imperfections on Zoom calls we'd all be happier.

I had an appointment with a South Dublin dermatologist years ago. I was probably around 37. This was the kind of dermatologist you find in a swanky clinic where everything is spotless and there is a hushed sense of doing important work. I was having a consultation with her for the red broken veins on my cheeks. She examined me and told me they could be solved with some IPL (Intense Pulsed Light Therapy), but while she was here, she said she would give me a whole face consultation. Eh, OK.

She told me that my face wasn't symmetrical (most people's faces aren't, except Brad Pitt and Angelina Jolie), that my right eyebrow had drooped slightly, but the good news was that it could be fixed by Botox – just a small amount to give it a lift. She then said I was lucky with my skin but that my 11s were going to become more pronounced and that I would be better off getting Botox now rather than waiting for them to get worse. She told me that my lips were thinning with age and drooping down either side of my jowls, making me look a little sad, but filler would help with that. Once all this was done, I'd look rested, fresh and happy. And if anyone asked about my fresh new look, I should tell them I've been drinking lots of water and that the baby is finally sleeping. True story.

I left there feeling a bit lopsided, but I soon realised that I don't want to try to look younger. Fresher, yes, I'd love that, but was I prepared to start something that I'd have to keep doing until … I died? And what happens as the years progress? And who was I really doing it for?

We are essentially being told that how we look is the most important thing about us (preferably young and wrinkle-free) BUT we are also told that it is our choice what we do. But is it really? If we are constantly being bombarded with before-and-after pics of women's faces being plumped and injected and poked to look younger and fresher, does this not send out the message that an ageing face is somehow unacceptable? I am suspicious of a whole industry that feeds off our insecurities. It never ends.

There is one thing I've done, though, and that is because, like a lot of women (I'm looking at you, Pamela Anderson), I plucked the bejaysus out of my eyebrows in my younger years. So I went and got PhiBrows – semi-permanent make-up on my eyebrows – that has helped fill in the area I plucked to death in my younger years (NEVER TOUCH YOUR EYEBROWS!). I go to Lizanne Proctor once a year for my top-up and otherwise don't have to think about them.

Decide what 'ageing well' means for you

We've all heard of the blue zones by now – these are regions where people live longer than average and maintain good health and where there are a particularly high number of centenarians. The reasons they give for these pockets of the world having populations of people living longer include a predominantly plant-based diet with lots of vegetables, a moderate calorie intake and low consumption of alcohol. These blue zones also place a very high value on family and social interaction and exercise is an integral part of life. So that suggests that eating a balanced diet, leading a healthy lifestyle and having a good social life are all crucial to ageing well.

There are, of course, lots of things here that we cannot help. Sickness can enter our lives and take away all choice in the matter, but there are lots of things we can do now in order to be as healthy as possible for as long as we do have that choice.

I hope to die healthy, as fit as I can be for the age that I am. So, to me that means lifting weights and stretching most mornings, getting out for a walk or a run most days and generally having a healthy diet. I have heard friends say that they just want to enjoy their life and what's the point being so good to just add on five years when you are so old? But I don't get that argument. I want to be able to spend my elder years doing the things I enjoy rather than being held back because I haven't looked after myself.

Ageing parents

All that being said, getting older is inevitable. I have friends with very elderly parents in their 90s who are still living healthy and independent lives, friends whose parents require full-time care and, of course, friends whose parents who did not see old age at all. One thing it's made me realise is that a little planning can go a long way.

It's a strange place to be; one day you are asking them for advice and the next you are the one minding them. We are all a little bit in denial about this whole process and most people don't want to have the difficult conversations. We wait until something happens to have THE TALK, but there are things you can discuss now that could help during difficult times. It can be as simple as sitting down over a cup of tea and asking your parents what their wishes would be in case of a medical emergency.

There is a thing called an Advanced Healthcare Directive, sometimes known as a living will. This is a legal document that spells out what medical treatments you would and would not want to be used to keep you alive, as well as other medical decisions such as pain management or organ donation. Having this document completed in advance means that should you be admitted to hospital, the doctors on duty can be easily made aware of your wishes in the case you are incapacitated and unable to communicate them. An Advanced Healthcare Directive template is available online and it's easy to fill out. This form should always be brought into the hospital with an elderly parent in case an emergency situation arises.

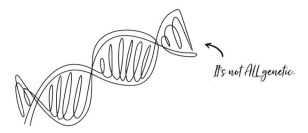

It's not ALL genetic.

Breaking the age code

And to end on a high, let me tell you about something I read not so long ago — a study by Becca Levy, Professor of Epidemiology at Yale University and author of *Breaking the Age Code*, found that having a positive outlook about ageing can add years to your life. The study followed hundreds of residents over the age of 50 in a small Ohio town and found that median survival was 7.5 years longer for those with the most positive beliefs about ageing compared with those who had the most negative attitudes. According to the research, looking forward to getting old also reduces the likelihood of heart disease, helps maintain strength and balance, reduces the likelihood of dementia and keeps your memory sharp. So, we all need to change the negative ageing narrative out there and instead look forward to our ageing years positively. Remember, only 25 per cent of our ageing health is determined by our genes!

YOU are the grown-up in your life now

M I've always felt older than I actually am. I was the baby of older parents (Mam was 40 and Dad was 42) and I have two much older sisters. I was always the youngest in my group of friends growing up. I generally only dated guys who were older than me too.

So, I thought I would be the youngest forever … but the fact is that ageing has managed to sneak up behind me, shout BOO and frighten the f**k out of me!

It feels like it's happened overnight. One minute I'm in the same age bracket (more or less) as hero and sports god Johnny Sexton, but now the Irish number 10, Jack Crowley, is young enough to be my son. I had the same feeling at a recent routine Garda tax and insurance checkpoint. I wanted to ask *them* for ID because they looked like children playing dress-up. I find it hard to believe that I am now 44 years old because I still feel like I'm growing up. Unfortunately, I *am* the grown-up in my life and I have seen the signs of ageing — some of which have appeared overnight:

- A hair on my chin that I thought belonged to my make-up brush, but it was ATTACHED to my face!

- The beginning of a bunion that's only going one way … wonky.

- Age spots that used to be cute freckles, and more lines.

- Black eyeliner always looked great on me, but now it looks weird.

- I need glasses to read everything – even texts.

- I need neck cream (more on that later).

- Arse cellulite – it's not going anywhere. It lives there now.

YOUR
LOOKS
ARE THE
LEAST
INTERESTING
THING
ABOUT YOU.

'Ageing well'

With three kids depending on me I know I need to look after myself and age well, but what does ageing well really mean?

- I exercise regularly, mainly weight training. I wish I could say I love going to classes, but I don't; I usually dread them but I feel great afterwards, so that's the reason I stick with them. This has been a revelation; I've always presumed the gym-goers loved gym-going ... but most of them don't! They go because they know they have to. I'm taking that on board now too and treating it like a job that has to be done. Do the laundry, vacuum the floor and get to the gym.

- I eat well – you don't need a list here, but I pack my diet with lots of fresh ingredients and I pay attention to sugar intake. I have to because I have a very large sweet tooth (or teeth).

- I drink very little alcohol, but I enjoy every drink I have.

- I don't smoke (never have) and I drink lots and lots of water.

All good, so I should live to be 105. But what will I look like? Well, if you look after the inside, you should look good on the outside too, right? Not always the case!

I was still getting spots at 40

As a former acne sufferer, I've tried every cream, lotion and facial out there. Some worked and cleared it up, but I constantly lived under the threat of a bad breakout. And of course, that would always happen in the run-up to some TV work, a wedding, a holiday or any big occasion. When I knew I was finished having children, I decided it was time to try Isotretinoin – more commonly known by its brand name, Roaccutane.

Roaccutane can only be prescribed by specialist dermatologists. Female patients must take the contraceptive pill alongside it because the drug may cause birth defects or stillbirths. A negative pregnancy test is also required before your dermatologist will prescribe the next month's dose.

I took this drug for seven months and it worked wonders for my persistent patchy acne. Overall, my complexion, including the areas that didn't have any acne, improved greatly too.

Before this, I had previously tried taking skin antibiotics in combination with using a topical treatment. They worked for a short time, but those big, sore red bumps would always reappear. Roaccutane is not for everyone – there are lots of things to consider – but if you are sick of getting spots in your thirties or forties then I recommend you talk to a dermatologist about it. It has been deemed one of the most effective drugs in treating acne, with a 95 per cent success rate in clearing up acne in four to six months. Around 70 per cent of those who take it say they never suffer from acne again. This was the main reason I went with it – to try to put an end to my skin troubles once and for all. And I can confirm that one year on from finishing treatment I am happily in the 70 per cent success bracket.

Want to keep that youthful face looking youthful?
Then STOP TANNING

We are all obsessed with lotions, potions, serums and creams, but the greatest thing you can do for your face is shade it.

- Stay out of the sun – it is the best anti-ageing 'treatment' out there and it's free.
- Wear SPF 50 on your face and neck – in fact, apply it all the way down to your boobies.
- Wear SPF 50 on your hands too. I started doing this in my late 30s (probably too late).
- Wear a hat and glasses – make yourself look like a really famous celeb who doesn't want their photo taken. Basically, be like Madonna on holiday.
- Remember the only safe tan you can get is a fake one.

I learned this lesson early on. At the age of 18 and on that first holiday without my parents, I suffered (oh GOD, did I suffer) from sunstroke. Day one, I decided that Gran Canaria was not that hot, so a low SPF 15 would do the job on my very pale skin. Some eight hours later, my skin was hot pink – I looked like a rasher with burnt eyelids. Later on, to add to the pain I was in from the burns, I began vomiting and developed a crushing headache. I spent the next three days in bed sipping water and slathering aftersun on my poor scorched and blistered skin. I didn't fully recover until I got home and I knew then that the tan life was not for me. Ever since then, I've been a sun dodger.

Treatments and tweakments

The rise of non-surgical cosmetic treatments – or, as they are now called, 'tweakments' – has gone through the roof. Many say it's because we all spent two years looking at ourselves on Zoom calls during the pandemic; others say it's because of Instagram. It's probably both, but it's also because they are now available to the masses. Many offer natural-looking results with no downtime required and they are (although still expensive) far more affordable than traditional cosmetic surgery. I differ to Jenny in my approach to ageing, in that I love a little intervention to give me a boost as long as it's nothing too extreme (see lip advice below)! Here's what has worked for me:

IPL – Intense Pulsed Light Therapy/Technology I've had IPL done a number of times to treat mild acne scarring and remove pigmentation, which I got a lot of while pregnant. But it can also be used to treat some broken veins, age spots, freckles and rosacea too. While I think I have a high pain threshold, I find this treatment really uncomfortable, but it's short, just 15 minutes, so I can bear the snapping pain in my face and neck. A topical numbing cream is applied to the area and there is also a built-in cooling system (it's a really cold fan you hold in the direction of your face while the professional does their thing). I have only had this done by a qualified nurse in a dermatology practice.

The wavelengths of light penetrate deep into the skin tissue to stimulate the cells beneath the skin's surface. This triggers the body's response to eliminate injured tissues and dead skin cells. The heat also stimulates new collagen production so after a number of treatments (usually three) you should have smoother, brighter, younger-looking skin.

Winter is the best time to get this done because you need to avoid sun exposure afterwards. I'm a fan because it's short — you are in and out in half an hour — and because it has worked for me.

Profhilo I did this once and actually couldn't cope with the level of compliments I got. You know that weird Irish thing where we can't take compliments? Well, they were coming from everywhere. Friends, family, even my dad! It made me think, 'God, I must have looked really awful last month.' So, if you are thinking about getting Profhilo, be prepared for a lot of 'your skin looks amazing' and some people may even try to touch your face.

What is Profhilo? It is a hyaluronic-acid-based product for treating skin laxity that is injected just under the skin. It targets lines, improving skin tone and texture. Skin looks really hydrated so it's perfect for those who don't want to get Botox and want to say, 'I've just been drinking lots of water.' This is what ALL the Hollywood heads do before award season to get that gorgeous, natural-looking glow. Warning: it does hurt a little, like multiple bee stings. This is a great one to do a few weeks out from a big occasion like a wedding. It is recommended that you get two treatments, four weeks apart, with results lasting between six and nine months. The downside is that it's spendy, at approximately €400 per treatment.

Advice on ageing lips

LEAVE THEM ALONE.

The end.

My everyday skincare routine

As well as the above, here's what works for me in terms of everyday skincare:

Cleanse As we mature (it's nicer than saying AGE) we need more hydrating cleansers. There are lots of great ones on the market. I have found since turning 40 that my preference has been to use cleansing balms. They melt make-up away, leaving my face feeling so clean and fresh. And the nighttime ritual of massaging it, then using a lukewarm soft cloth to remove it, just signals to my brain that it's sleepy time.

- My favourite cleanser: Nunaïa Superfood Cleansing Balm (Guide price €59)

- Best budget option: Ella & Jo Melt the Day Away Cleansing Balm (Guide price €28)

Toner: the superhero product in my bathroom

- My favourite toner: Biologique Recherche Lotion P50. I've used this for years and it is probably the only thing Kim Kardashian and myself have in common. She is a huge fan of this skin care brand. The P stands for 'peeling' and the 50 represents two epidermal cycles. I use P50 PIGM 400 – it exfoliates, reduces pigmentation and hydrates all at the same time. It's like a facial in a bottle. I use this once a day, every day. But I can't recommend this one for you because there are four different P50 lotions to choose from. My advice would be to talk to a stockist who will advise you correctly – what has worked for me might be disastrous for you. (Guide price €125)

- Best budget option: The Ordinary Glycolic Acid 7% toning solution. This is an exfoliator that smoothes skin texture and, with regular use, can create a more even skin tone too. (Guide price €13)

Eye creams are like pensions –
START YOUNG

I don't have deep lines around my eyes. I think that's because I've stayed out of the sun, because of my genetics and because I haven't laughed enough? Or maybe it's because I started using eye cream when I was just 20 years old. I started with the Body Shop eye gel, clear in colour with no scent, but I loved how my eyes felt after I put a pea-sized amount on each night.

Now I've upped my eye game:

- **My favourite eye cream:** Skinceuticals A.G.E eye complex cream. This is very spendy at roughly €100 for 15ml (I've paid between €90 and €115 at different times). While some might think this is an enormous amount to spend on a small jar of eye cream, I ask: have you ever gone into Penneys or Zara to buy nothing and yet come out with two bags of stuff worth €150? Yes, you have ... We have only two eyes and they will still be on your face and in your head long after the Penneys pyjama set and the Zara tops are gone, so I figure it's worth it. Use a very small amount, it goes a long way. And only use your ring finger to apply. I also love Irish brand Seabody's Pentabrite eye serum. Because this is a serum, it has a completely different texture to the Skinceuticals cream, but it is absorbed beautifully. (Guide price €86)

- **Best budget option:** It's hard to beat CeraVe Eye Repair Cream. A really lovely eye cream; start here if you've never used one before. (Guide price €15–€17)

Eye Magic

Start early!

Let's talk about NECKS, baby

As the great Nora Ephron said, we need to 'start hiding our necks from the age of 43, because our faces are lies but our necks are the truth'.

Well, not anymore, because I found the most delicious neck cream. I ordered some items from a pharmacy, and they threw in a few samples of some other items (this is a sales technique that obviously works). One of the samples was a neck cream. I thought, 'How odd, surely a face cream is the same as a neck cream?' Wrong! It's Neostrata Triple Firming Neck Cream (guide price €78–€80). A really rich moisturiser that firms and tones the skin on your neck. After using the small sample, I purchased a bottle and I have continued to use it since. My neck is much smoother and softer, but tighter, and now I don't feel bad about my neck at all, Nora.

Thinning hair

While you may have hair sprouting out of your chin, nipples, toes or nostrils (or all of the above!) the hair on your head starts to thin as we age due to hormone changes.

I have started wearing two small, taped hair extensions on the sides of my head. I use London Hair Lab which, despite the name, is an Irish company. I go about my days not knowing they are there, because they are THAT comfortable to wear. Many women might feel that hair extensions are just for the Insta Huns with waist-length locks, but using a very small number of good-quality hair extensions can help fill out thinning sides. And when your hair is still swishy-swishy, you will look and feel better. (If you want to read more about hair, we have an entire chapter coming on all things hair, from products to tools!)

What I know now about ageing is that it's all about acceptance. And while I genuinely accept who I am, I, like many women reading this now, will continue to not accept what ageing is doing to me. And so, I'll tweak:

- I've accepted that I have grey hair – but I'll dye it blonde for now.

- I've accepted my pale white skin – but it's not porcelain enough to be shown, so I'll fake-tan it.

- I've accepted that my already small lips will get smaller – but I will leave them alone.

EYE
CREAMS
ARE LIKE
PENSIONS —
START
YOUNG.

What we know now about ↘

joy

OR, WHY YOU NEED TO GET A DOG

Staring at trees can make you happier than owning that Mulberry handbag

M **We are all searching for 'happiness'. Often we think, 'When I get the promotion I'll be happy, when I have a partner I'll be happy, when I lose weight I'll be happy.' But happiness and joy are not a summit you can ever reach if you keep moving your happiness goal posts further and further away. Happiness is not the finish line that you cross at the end of a race; it's all the lovely stuff that happens along the way every day. If you pause your happiness until the 'when' happens, you will *always* be disappointed.**

I feel like I spent a decade on the finding happiness treadmill, always on an incline trying to hit the next joyful mile. Thinking I'll be happier if I get that job on telly, I'll be happier when we go on holidays, I'll be happier when we get a mortgage ... I'll be happier if and when blah blah happens!

One thing Jenny and I have learned is that what brings you joy will change through the decades. What brings me joy now and what I thought would bring me joy when I was younger are very different, but then I suppose that's the joy of maturity. Take, for example, this list of what gave us joy in the past — it would now be our worst nightmare.

Joy in our 20s

- Very late nights out in Lillie's nightclub followed by a 3 a.m. McDonald's (which was conveniently next door). Then an easily found taxi home was the joyous cherry on the cake.

- Planning the next night out straight after the last night out.

- Working very hard with no concept of logging off or saying no to an opportunity (we were very lucky to have genuinely loved our jobs every single day in radio).

- Wearing heels.

- Designer bags – both of our first ones were Prada and we still love them, BUT we know now that owning multiple designer handbags is not where joy lies. Being out in nature, staring up at a cherry blossom tree, wins hands down in the joy stakes (and it's a lot less expensive).

- Being with people ALL THE TIME.

Mairéad used to say that high heels never hurt her and she wore them ALL the time in work and there was a lot of running around. She was in her 20s then and had magic feet that felt no heel pain. **J**

What brings us joy now

We have to follow that list with what brings us both joy now. Our younger selves would pity us and think, 'Ah, God love them, the poor bitches … they are soooooo boring.'

- Someone handing you a dinner you didn't have to cook yourself.

- The goodnight kiss and tucking in our kids when they are asleep each night.

- Walking the dog alone.

- The 'Ta-dum' sound of the Netflix logo as you finally sit down in the evening to watch something.

- Getting a great parking spot.

- The text from your teen that says 'Mum, I'm home' when they stay over at a friend's house.

- Cleaning – THE JOY. Cleaning is the ONLY thing that brings me close to a meditative state. I've tried listening to guided meditations and I can't do it. But when I'm cleaning my home, I feel like my brain goes quiet, my thoughts become still and I start to relax … and the bonus is the house looks amazing afterwards.)

  My spray mop is my spiritual friend – it's the tsss, tsss noise as it sprays and the mopping motion that does it for me – I am Zen. J

- Going to bed early with a good book.

- Keeping plants alive (Jenny has nearly killed the same hydrangea plant a few times but like Lazarus it keeps coming back to life).

- A summer dip in the sea with a friend.

- Wearing Birkenstocks.

- Those precious moments when our teenagers actually want to spend time with us.

- Owning your own time.

- Lighting smelly candles – we recommend spendy (but worth it) brand La Bougie or Irish brand Brooke and Shoals. Dunnes do a huge selection of smelly candles with a smell for everyone.

- A square of 85% dark chocolate (the treat of queens!) with a cup of tea or over a catch-up with a good friend. My tea must have the teabag in it for AGES, then the teabag squeezed, and then a tiny drop of milk added. It should resemble the colour of fake tan coming right out of the bottle … beautiful!

Mairéad takes the most bizarre amount of milk in hers – half a teaspoon. God forbid if you give her more than that. And I like builder's tea – nice and strong. J

It's just a suggestion of milk!

And since we both love tea

J Here is something to think about the next time you are making yourself a cup.

Thich Nhat Hanh was a Vietnamese Zen Buddhist Monk who wrote many books and lived a life of such beautiful purpose and simplicity that we could all do with taking time out to read his teachings. One of his life lessons is about how making and drinking tea holds the key to a simple, joyous life. When you are making tea, make the tea. When you are drinking tea, drink your tea. In other words, let the world outside fade away for the moments you are making the tea, no thoughts of future or past. Let go of lists of things to do or arguments to fixate on and just make the tea. Once the tea is made, sit and enjoy the moment: savour the taste, the warmth of the mug in your hands. This, he tells us, is the act of life, letting go of drama and pain. Just this moment, nothing else. And since we both drink approximately eight cups of tea a day, that gives us at least eight times throughout the day to stop and feel the joy.

A nice thing to do in these moments is to write down some of the things that bring you joy — so make that cup of tea and take a pen and piece of paper out. Seeing it written down in front of you will make you smile.

Holiday heaven? Or hell?

Ahh, holidays — a time to relax and enjoy a well-deserved rest. Where you get to spend time with your family and have adventures. A time to experience different cultures and destinations. A time to soak up some sun and try new foods. Sounds like heaven. But a lot of the time, the experience is very different to the dream. But why is that? I think it's because our expectations are far too high. If you are a family of four, all different ages with different expectations of a holiday, I think it's a recipe for disaster. You are stressed before you even get to the airport. If you are the mum (yes, I said mum, because 99 per cent of the time it is the mum) you have probably booked the holiday after hours of research, stressing over making sure everyone's needs are catered for; you have booked flights; washed and packed everyone's clothes; shopped for toiletries; cleaned the entire house ready for your return; booked the dog into the kennels; booked the taxi or parking for the airport; organised entertainment for the kids for when they are on the plane; sorted out the transfer from the airport to the hotel or apartment ... by the time you actually get to your destination, you are fit for bed! And then if there is any moaning about your choices you, of course, take it very personally!

I think we need to lower our holiday expectations. We build this one or two weeks up so much that it is going to be almost impossible to feel satisfied. Most of us look forward to our holidays, but one of the best bits of going away is coming home again, isn't it? It's getting on the plane and thinking of getting into your own lovely bed that evening. Home sweet home.

LET GO OF
LISTS OF
THINGS
TO DO OR
ARGUMENTS
TO FIXATE
ON AND
JUST MAKE
THE TEA.

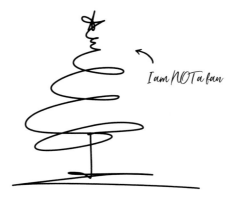

I am NOT a fan

The C Word

And while we are here talking about holidays, can we talk about 'the C word'?

Yes, I'm talking about CHRISTMAS. I am not a fan. I know that is a controversial statement to make, but I think a lot of women secretly feel this way, because Christmas is hard work. We hear again and again that Christmas is all about spending time with family and cosying up at home, but the reality is a lot of women running around, spinning half a dozen plates. There is the big food shop, the shopping for all the gifts (and wrapping them), getting the house all Christmassy, booking pantos and Santa visits and on, and on, and on. Oh, and making sure there is enough hot chocolate to collapse a small European country. And DO NOT FORGET MARSHMALLOWS. The pressure makes me want to cry. I am so happy when January comes along. I love the having to do nothing of January; I love the weather, the early dark days, the cosiness of having the stove lit and having nowhere to go. This, to me, is heaven. This to me is family holiday time (and Mairéad agrees with ALL of this. Christmas is a gigantic pain for women!).

#makingmemories

(M) This generation of parents are under so much pressure. From trying to work full time, to finding an affordable place to live, and throw in childcare costs, too ... and on top all of that stress, they are also carrying the burden of trying to #makememories with their kids with any downtime they have. It seems to be a constant stream of plans: play-dates, trips to the park, the zoo, the cinema, the panto, hot chocolates, treats, pizza night and swimming (my favourite!), when actually most kids are so busy with homework and their after-school activities that they probably just want to do nothing at home. Doing nothing and going nowhere in your downtime is completely normal!

Maybe this pressure to #makememories is because it's so easy for us to capture them on camera and share with the world. We've all seen some beautifully shot Instagram reels; I'm guilty of creating the odd one myself.

But when I look back, I have an abundance of really happy memories of spending time with my mother when I was a child. I have vivid images in my head of us having lunch every day at a tiny table by the cooker in the months before I started primary school. I remember her always allowing me to lick the whisk once she had finished whipping cream every Sunday, or sitting beside her in my little chair by the fire. I have no memories with my mam at a beach because Maureen thought they were always 'too breezy', and I never went to the cinema with her — ever, because she would fall asleep in the dark. There

Sunday treat

were no bouncy castles or any big fanfare birthday parties, but I was consistently content, because I had her and I knew I was adored by her. My favourite memories are all from home. So, we all need to ease up on the pressure to make every weekend FULL with things to do and places to go. Kids don't need much, despite us being bombarded with ads telling us they do.

Recently my middle child told me that her favourite day this year was 'the day we didn't get dressed'. That sounds like we went around naked – we didn't. Instead, we stayed in our PJs for the whole day and then put fresh ones on going to bed that night. Although all children are unique, they are all kind of the same, too; they just want their parents and their home. Let's normalise doing nothing with our kids and their free time.

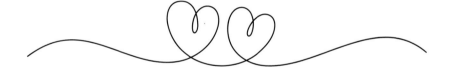

Speaking of joy ... dogs are pure love

We always had dogs growing up in our house. We had Brandy the Red Setter, Toby the Pomeranian/Pekingese mix, Charlie the Tibetan Spaniel and Ben the Jack Russell. I love dogs. I love their faces, their squishy paws and their unique personalities. They make a house a home. My husband grew up in a house with no animals (there were nine kids!) and so couldn't understand my need for a dog. He was quite right that we were too busy to take care of a dog; we were working all the time and at that stage had a four-year-old child who needed all of our attention. I understood that practically speaking it was a mad thing to do, but I still wanted a dog nonetheless. And then my dad died suddenly and all bets were off. 'Why wait?' I thought. Anything could happen at any time: we had to do it now before it was too late (that's what I told myself, anyway).

Choosing your spirit animal

The story of how I chose our first family dog goes back to a trip I took to Nepal in 2002. While hiking there I came across this gorgeous breed of dog called Lhasa Apso. Originally from Tibet, they were used as an inside guard dog, protecting the homes of Tibetan people and Buddhist monasteries. They were also believed to have spiritual powers and were thought to bring good luck and fortune to their owners. I loved their cheeky faces and thought that out of all the dogs out there, this was the breed I was meant to get (there was also a part of me that thought my dad could be reincarnated in one of them — I realise that sounds completely bats, but sudden death does strange things to a person). I found a woman in Tipperary who bred Lhasas and got in touch, and a few months later travelled to her home to pick up Teddy. Oh, Teddy, the loveliest dog ever (Mairéad will have something to say on this, I'm sure).

Yes, Murphy is prettier!
Ⓜ

Teddy is stubborn and very lazy. Like me, his favourite place to be is his bed. He snores like a rhinoceros and only does what he wants to do. I love him for this. And to answer your question, I am not sure if my dad was reincarnated in him, but sometimes when I look at him I think, maybe ... Teddy is 12 now. He is blind and sleeps most of the day. But he rules the roost.

And then there is Stanley, also known as Handsome Stan. Have you ever seen the film *Marley & Me*? Owen Wilson and Jennifer Aniston adopt a Golden Retriever puppy who wrecks their house and behaves so badly he gets kicked out of doggy obedience school. Stanley is a bit like that ... only worse. I have never in all my years been tested as much by a dog. The only reason he is still around is because he is the most handsome dog in Ireland. Honestly, it's like hanging around with a supermodel; when I take him outside people stop me and say, 'Oh my God, he is so beautiful,' and I smile and look bashful and thank them – as if I had something to do with it!

Ray tried to warn me. He pointed out that I like a very clean home and that Golden Retrievers shed like mad and bring dirt in, lots of it. I did not listen. He pointed out that we had a three-year-old son, an eight-

After

year-old daughter, full-time jobs and another dog. I did not listen. I went ahead and got Stanley. The first thing I remember about him was the size of his paws. They were ENORMOUS. HUGE. MAHOOSIVE. 'Eh, how big is this dog going to get?' I wondered. 'Very big,' is the answer.

Before

Who knew that so much poo could come out of a little puppy? Who knew that so many shoes and rugs and cushions could be eaten? Who knew how many holes could be dug in the garden, how many ways out of our garden he would find, how many pees on rugs and farts stinking up the surrounding air ... all from one puppy? Nothing will wake you up quicker than coming downstairs in the morning after a good night's sleep only to step on a large liquid poo in the kitchen. I woke up most mornings to hear retching noises coming from my husband. I thought he might divorce me. 'He'll grow out of it,' I said confidently, while slyly googling 'When do Golden Retrievers grow up?' He is now eight. I'm still waiting.

I tell people he is my spiritual practice. I am a very impatient person and I have been tested on so many occasions with this dog. And yet ... I love him very, very much. Ray says that I tell the dog how handsome he is a lot more than I say it to him. It's true. I realise this is bad. But his face! Ray has even come on board with the dog love. When I ask him now if he loves them, he says, 'I tolerate them.' But I know that deep down he loves them.

Last year there was a TikTok post that went viral — a woman said that a stranger had just offered her €200,000 to buy her Doberman Pinscher puppy. She said that she told her husband no way would she do it, that it would be like 'selling her child'. As you can imagine, this exploded online. Soon after I heard Ray talking about it on his radio show. He was on the fence about whether he'd do it or not. I actually texted in to the show to say that I was outraged that he would even consider it. I'm with the woman who said it would be like selling her child! Your dog becomes part of the family. They *are* family. There is no way on this earth I would sell them (as much as I've thought about it with Stanley).

Never, ever, going to be a bad idea.

Reasons to get a dog

- They are pure goodness and love. Even if no one else is happy to see you, a dog will welcome you home like no one else.

- It will force you outside into nature (if you need forcing). Dogs need exercise and you will have to walk them.

- On that note, be prepared to meet the nicest people you will ever meet when out with your dog, because dog people are amazing. There is nothing I like better than asking someone else about their dog and telling them how fab their dog is. Their faces always light up (the humans', not the dogs').

- Dogs are emotionally intuitive. They will know when you are sad and will come over and nuzzle you. Unless they're Teddy, who will just ignore you, but that's just Teddy.

- Dogs will bring joy to your life. Yes, they are hard work. Yes, you need to give them a lot of time and energy, but you will get a million per cent more back in love and adoration. The way they look at you is pure love.

- Dogs make a house a home. Young children who grow up with dogs are so lucky. And by the way, just in case your kids are begging for a dog and tell you that they will mind it and pick up its poo – they are lying, you will end up doing it all. That is just a fact. But dogs are smart and they know that the woman is the alpha and so they will shower you in love (and hair and slobber).

- Because dogs are the best – we don't deserve them.

RAY SAYS
THAT I
TELL THE
DOG HOW
HANDSOME
HE IS A LOT
MORE THAN
I SAY IT TO
HIM.
IT'S TRUE.

But HE ATE MY SHOES – a dog-owning reality check

But (there is always a but) having a dog is a lot of work. Animal shelters are packed with unwanted animals because their owners did not take the time to think through the reality of keeping a pet. You bring an animal into your home and find that they dig up your garden, wreck your house and chew your shoes. They have to be house trained and they cost a lot to keep with food and vet bills. You can't just head away when you want, you have to find a minder or kennels that you trust, and this costs a lot of money. Dogs live for on average 10 to 13 years, so think about all those years that you are going to be responsible for this animal. Sometimes it's better to understand the negatives of doing something before imagining all the positives. Maybe try fostering or pet-sitting first to see if this is something that suits you and your family life. Or look after a friend's pet while they are away to get a handle on the realities of caring for an animal. Maybe start small, with a goldfish or hamster, and see how the commitment to an animal sits with your family. If you are struggling to take care of a fish then, most certainly, a dog is not for you. But like with most things, if you are determined to take care of a pet then you will figure it out, and they will become like a family member who you could not imagine living without.

It's not all about dogs

And I can't just talk about dogs. When I was growing up, we had lots of animals – goldfish, hamsters and guinea pigs, rabbits, a cat and horses – so if you are not a dog person there's loads more options for you. I am a lover of all animals. My dream is to live in the countryside with some land around me and have all the animals I've listed above – and I'll throw in some donkeys, chickens, geese, pigs (I love pigs), goats, and maybe even a few sheep. Will that happen? Maybe one day.

Love is a four-legged word

(M) I had to wait until I was 35 years old to get my first dog. Louis and I were newlyweds in a big love bubble, and it seemed like the perfect time to get a dog. Plus, I was producing the *Ian Dempsey Breakfast Show* on Today FM and got home each day before 2 p.m. (these things are important if you have a pet).

Louis wanted a Jack Russell but his last one, Moses, didn't really like anyone other than Louis so that was a hard 'no' from me.

I suggested to him that we should get the same dog as Jenny, a Lhasa Apso (which is kind of the opposite of a Jack Russell), because they look like they belong on a shelf in Smyths Toys. Jenny's dog Teddy was a beauty back in the day. Now he's like Geoge Clooney, still gorgeous but past his peak.

And so we went to the same breeder that Jenny went to for Teddy. We brought home Murphy – who is Teddy's nephew! Let me explain: Teddy is the brother of Murphy's dad.

Growing up we weren't allowed to have pets. They were deemed too expensive, too much work and they would eventually break your heart. Murphy is my mam's maiden name. I named him after her because I want to let her know that I can afford a dog, I'm OK with hard work and I've had my heart broken and survived. I was ready... ish! I knew nothing other than the basic things a dog needs: food, walks and love.

And, oh my God, did we fall in love.

Murphy is so beautiful, he walks like he should have a Disney theme song playing in the background and has the most gorgeous personality. I'm pretty sure he was here in this life before. There have been so many nights when the kids are in bed and I've made myself tea and got three biscuits. Then, when I've gone to get more of said biscuits, Murphy STARES at me – with his deep brown eyes – like he's saying, 'No, don't, Mairéad; the answer to your problems is not at the end of the packet of biscuits.' Call me crackers, but I know he understands more than 'sit', 'stay', 'walk' and 'treat'. Here are some of the best things about Murphy:

- When I had a miscarriage, he stayed on the bed with me so I could rub his gorgeous coat and feel comforted. He didn't leave the room unless I did.

- When any of the kids are off sick, he will stay close to them.

- He's a trip hazard every time I cook, hovering at my feet just hoping something will fall, so I fully believe quick steps over him with hot food gave me years of pre-training for *Dancing with the Stars*.

- He has a special, different bark just for the fox that comes into our garden every night at 9.30 p.m.

- He can do a few tricks – my favourite is when I ask him to show me his teeth and he flashes his Hollywood smile.
- Each time I come home he behaves like I've just come back from four years in Australia (but I've just popped up to SuperValu). His happiness at seeing us is infectious, and even if I've arrived home grumpy, Murphy's reaction lifts my mood.

There is expense in having a dog (Murphy's haircuts cost €80) but there is so much loneliness in Ireland at the moment. Dogs can take a heap of that away. They can't talk, obviously, but they can communicate and they are so full of love. They get their owners out every single day regardless of the weather, and while they sniff another dog's bum, you just have to stand there and chat with the other dog owner.

'Dogs' lives are too short.

Their only fault, really.

AGNES SLIGH TURNBULL
WRITER

What we know now about

alcohol

OR, HOW TO LIVE THAT SPARKLY LIFE

Locked, pickled and pie-eyed

J If you listen to our podcast you will know that I have a name for the mean voice in my head. I call her Jane. She is a wagon who tries to make me doubt myself and feel fear. Well, there is another voice in there too and it is a voice with no name. She is calm and quiet and whispery. I find it difficult to hear her sometimes, especially when I'm busy and filling up my time with lots of things to keep myself from thinking. But she persists ... and eventually I have to listen to her.

Around eight years ago, this voice started telling me in a kind and gentle way that alcohol was not my friend. That was it. Nothing else too profound, just that one sentence: 'Alcohol is not your friend.' Initially I dismissed it. I assumed it was just 'the fear' after a night out trying to make me feel bad. So I continued to push the voice away for over two years until I couldn't ignore it anymore.

Was it true? Was alcohol not my friend anymore? Or maybe it was worse than that; maybe alcohol had never been my friend at all. I was pretty devastated. How on earth would I live without alcohol in my life? How would I socialise, commiserate, celebrate, have downtime, go on holidays ... how would I have a life at all? I'd end up just being miserable forever and becoming the most boring person in the whole of Ireland. Yes, I was that dramatic. But that was honestly how I felt.

For nearly 30 years I had drunk alcohol and now I was having an internal fight with myself as to whether or not I should stop. People always want to know why. Did I have a problem? Was I an alcoholic? It's as if people believe that there must have been a BIG problem to even contemplate something so drastic as stopping drinking alcohol. The truth is complicated. I was brought up surrounded by alcohol. It was everywhere. Every adult drank and every social situation had alcohol included. I never thought about not drinking. I thought it was the same as breathing – you just did it. Once I started drinking, I thought it made me more fun and interesting. I thought it made EVERYTHING more fun and interesting. And it was fun for quite some time. Until it wasn't. And did I mention the anxiety? The FEAR. I got it bad. Like VERY BAD. So not only was it a hangover of feeling sick with a headache, I also had a feeling of utter doom and despair. Imagine that – a depressant was making me feel depressed! I began to ask myself why I was doing this to myself. Was this it? Drinking, feeling hungover, getting better and then doing it all again on repeat, forever?

I wanted to find out for myself whether there was a life to be had without alcohol in it. Was that possible? So I read every book on going sober out there, read many articles and listened to podcasts. I felt like I was deprogramming myself from years and years of conditioned thinking. I challenged myself and my thoughts. It was a very interesting time. And then in July 2018, in the middle of summer, I stopped. I didn't tell anyone except my husband, and I quietly got on with doing it day by day. Was it easy? Was it hell! It was very, very hard. I basically lived like a hermit for 6 months, too scared to go out in case anyone asked me if I wanted a drink. This was a huge preoccupation for me – what would I say if I was asked whether I wanted a drink? It seems funny now, but at the time I was a little bit terrified.

I could honestly write a whole book about the process instead of one little chapter, but instead I've put together points that I think give you the full(ish) story of what it's like to give up alcohol after 30 years of drinking while living in a booze-soaked country in which stopping drinking immediately means YOU are the one with the problem.

My whole life I'd been programmed to see alcohol as something that added to my life

Alcohol, in fact, made me loud and careless about others. I did things and said things that I'm not proud of. I kind of think of it like the Jim Carrey movie *The Mask* — after I had that first drink it was like I put on the mask of booze and my personality revved up by 200 per cent. Let me tell you, no one needs their personality revved up by 200 per cent. It's too much. I am not a fan of that version of me and I'm so glad that the mask has been put away for good.

I used to believe that you were either a 'normal' drinker or an alcoholic

Until I realised that there is a whole spectrum on which you can find yourself. In fact, believing in 'normal' and 'alcoholic' harms people as it makes you believe that you are OK, you are not that bad, you have not yet reached that rock bottom. To realise you don't have to reach a rock bottom is a life-altering moment. You can just decide you have had enough.

For the first time in my 30-year drinking history I quietly sat and examined my relationship with alcohol. I had so many false beliefs such as: alcohol made me social and fun, it relaxed me, when I was sad it made me happy (it didn't) or when I was happy it made me even happier (it didn't, it actually muted my feelings). So many contradictions.

My biggest fear was telling people.

This was huge for me. I felt like I might as well go out naked with a large sign hanging around my neck with ALCO written on it. When the first event came around after I spent the first few months living like a hermit, I was met with sadness that I wasn't going to be participating in the fun day. It was supposed to be a boozy lunch and here was I with my fizzy water dampening the whole atmosphere. I was that person that no one wants out — a non-drinker!

It's here that I'm going to put in a few tips for you if a friend in your group decides they are going to stop drinking:

- Don't tell them they are boring or over the top.
- Do say something like 'Oh that's interesting, tell me all about it on our walk.'
- Don't pull a sad face and keep reminiscing about all your booze-soaked fun times together.
- Do say, 'Can I get you a sparkling water?'
- Don't assume they will forever be the designated driver.
- Do make a decision not to always meet for drinks out or boozy dinners – try different venues like coffee shops, the outdoors, the cinema ... not everything should revolve around booze.
- Don't tilt your head to the side and say, 'So you're an alcoholic, then.'
- Do ask for book recommendations if you are sober-curious.
- Don't take offence when they stop wanting to go out to boozy locations to watch a gang of you get pissed.
- Do keep inviting your non-drinking friend out. They are not judging you (they will, however, more often than not, say no if it's just the pub you are going to).

(I'll always remember when I told Mairéad that I had stopped drinking. She just nodded and said, 'Oh yeah, you're done,' and it was the best reaction from anyone ever, because she just got it. I was done.)

Give yourself a booze reality-check

If you do decide to stop drinking, keep giving yourself a reality check because it is easy to go off in your head, remembering all the wonderful boozy highs of days and nights gone by ... Remind yourself of the reality: the wasted days of hangovers, the panic and anxiety, narkiness, sadness, mortification, fear and upset. I once read something that struck a chord with me — place all your messy boozy memories in an imaginary photo album and, when you are remembering your great fun nights out, just let yourself slowly turn the pages in your head of what really happened as the night went on. You'll soon close your imaginary booze photo album and put the kettle on.

But I'm so bloody boring now! Really? As opposed to when you were repeating yourself for the third time, shouting and slurring your words and spending money you didn't have on slippery nipples? Those crazy nights out might be looked back at through a haze of wistful thinking about all the fun we had in our 20s (and a lot of them were mad fun times), but as I got older, the price that had to be paid for those nights out was far too high — and it wasn't costing me money, but fear and anxiety.

How will I ever go on holidays again if I don't drink? Is it even really a holiday if you can't drink? How many times have you gone on holidays, drunk more than you normally do every single day, and come home nearly needing another holiday to start feeling normal again? The difference to my life now is that I come home from holidays feeling like I've had one. I come home rested and relaxed and full of beans. This is why we go on holidays, to recharge and give ourselves some self-care and rest. Think about that.

Alcohol gives you false confidence

It's probably one of the main reasons why you started drinking in the first place. But it is false. We have been tricked from an early age by the alcohol industry to believe that we 'need' alcohol, that it makes us better, funnier, happier, sexier. Cigarette companies did this for years until people finally realised that they were being duped. The alcohol industry tells us to 'drink responsibly', which is a laugh – it is an addictive drug, meaning it's not your fault that you end up wanting more and more. We think that alcohol is the elixir of life, the drug that makes us acceptable. But sit with your thoughts, and if there is a teeny–tiny voice in your head telling you that alcohol is not your friend, pay attention. This is your true self reminding you that you are enough, you don't need anything to make you any better. You are perfect just as you are (as an Irish person I know this is hard to believe).

The Big C

There seems to be a complete disconnect or at least ignorance of the fact that alcohol has a direct link to at least seven cancers, including breast, mouth, oesophageal, stomach, bowel and liver. Ironically, I've seen breast cancer charities hosting champagne receptions as fundraisers. The World Health Organisation has said, 'No level of alcohol consumption is safe for our health', and alcohol is classified as a Group 1 carcinogen (this is a high–risk group which also includes asbestos, radiation and tobacco). This is not scaremongering; these are just facts, and facts give us power and choice.

Just one of the lads

In the 1990s women were sold the lie of the 'ladette' — we were told that we could be just like the lads and drink as much as them. We can't, and we shouldn't. Unfortunately, this continues to this day with women being directly targeted by the alcohol industry. How many kitchens have you been in where you see a 'funny' sign on the wall that says, 'It's not drinking alone if the dog is home', or t-shirts with a pic of a wine glass and written underneath, 'Mummy's wine because kids whine'. I can tell you one thing: the last thing a mum needs is a feed of wine when she is finding things tough at home with kids — she needs sleep and minding and self-care. More and more young women are presenting with liver disease; this is a silent and deadly illness, one that we don't fear because we don't hear about it until it's too late.

It's not you, it's me (well, really it's you)

I wasn't prepared to lose contact with quite so many people once I ditched the booze. So much of socialising in Ireland involves alcohol. I was asked in a jokey way why I couldn't start drinking again, I was told that I was no craic anymore, that I had changed so much ... I was even asked on one night out with a bunch of friends if they could have the 'old Jenny back for one night only'. Now, luckily for me, I had everything clear in my head to be able to brush off these comments, but I can't say it was easy. There is probably no worse insult from an Irish person than being told you are 'boring' and 'no craic'. I began to think that our only connection had been booze and that I was making them feel very uncomfortable by not drinking. It was like I was holding a mirror up to them for their drinking and they did not like that. So, I stopped, sat back and really allowed myself to think and feel about the things I liked to do and whom I liked doing these things with. I learned to ask myself what I wanted to do rather than getting caught up in what others wanted. I gave myself permission to be my own best friend.

DECIDING TO
STOP DRINKING
ALCOHOL
HAS BEEN
THE MOST
ENLIGHTENING,
POSITIVE,
JOYFUL,
LIFE-CHANGING
THING I'VE
EVER DONE.

A sparkly life

Deciding to stop drinking alcohol has been the most enlightening, positive, joyful, life-changing thing I've ever done. I never thought this would be me, but I am so glad that I paid attention to that little voice inside my head all those years ago. I thought that I was living my best life – how wrong I was. I feel as if I've woken up. Everything is so much shinier and brighter. Life feels sparkly and vibrant. And before I burst into song, of course I have off days when the shine has somewhat diminished, but that's when all my self-care techniques kick in. I feel my feelings, I allow them in and make myself a cup of tea with a purple Snack bar – far better than a glass of wine or beer would have ever done for me. I'm no longer numb to both the good and bad. I am living a real life. Cheers!

And now for something completely different ...

M I really respect and admire Jenny's approach to alcohol and support her all the way, but I'm a drinker and still really enjoy drinking. I'm partial to a cold glass of savvy b, or in winter some rioja, or at any time of the year a zesty gin and tonic. But my relationship with alcohol has changed a lot over the last eight years.

Like so many Irish people, alcohol was a huge part of my life in my 20s and the first half of my 30s. It was an intense, full-on friend who I needed to have with me at every gig, every match, every date and every night out that I went on. And I loved every one of those nights because I remember all of them. Forgive me if I sound like 'head girl' here, but I was never the worst in the gang. How I drank then was different to how others in my group did – I was always measured even in the madness – although my aim was the same as everyone else's: go out, get drunk, have a laugh, die with a hangover the next day and say thank you, next. My standard recovery was chips.

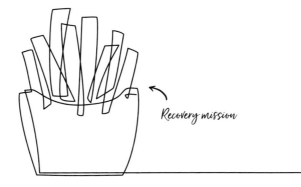

Recovery mission

Kids
+
less sleep
+
alcohol
=
grumpy bitch mum

When my second child Eliza was born, Dara (my first) was nine years old. I was going back to baby-land and had totally forgotten how much work little people are. When I eventually had a drink again, it was as if my tolerance for alcohol had completely vanished. Of course it had! I was older, I was a really busy mum with two kids (both with very different needs) AND I was sleep deprived. If I had a few drinks I found that the next day I was snappy, moany, slow, a bit dopey and generally a grumpy bitch. This is not what any child needs from their mum or dad. So measured Mairéad became ... even more measured. I didn't cut drink out because I didn't feel I needed to or wanted to, but I copped on.

My attitude now

This will sound very simplistic and I'm not suggesting anyone else agree with this, but I look at alcohol the same way I look at chocolate. I love the taste of chocolate so much (God, I really love chocolate) but I can't have it all the time, because if I do, I will gain weight, wreck my teeth, get spots, increase my risk of heart disease and type 2 diabetes and ultimately I'll feel shit.

With alcohol, I enjoy the taste of my favourites and I enjoy the social aspect, but again I can't have it too often — nor do I want to — because I know if I do I will feel anxious, get bloated, gain weight, have my sleep interrupted and put myself at higher risk of some cancers.

Staying with the chocolate analogy — at Easter time I'll eat ALL of the chocolate eggs until they're gone. And if we go on holidays, I'll probably have some small amount of alcohol everyday ... but that does not continue when we return home.

As I write this, I realise I haven't had any alcohol for over three weeks (looking at my calendar, it's 24 days since I was last out) but I'm not a non-drinker and I'm not sure I ever will be. Who knows ... I say that because when I drink, I enjoy every one I have, but as soon as I feel I'm veering towards woozy I stop — because anything after woozy is not fun.

Alcohol has gone from being that friend who I saw LOTS of and stayed out very late with to now being a pal I enjoy hooking up with every now and again for a coffee ... or maybe a cheese board.

Managing a big night out

If I'm out for a big night I always alternate my drinks — so I'll flit between a gin and tonic, and then the next round just a tonic (hold off on the gin). There are loads of really great offerings on the market now, too.

Tastiest mocktail ever

It's hard to beat a virgin mojito because you get all of the taste and none of the damage.

> 1 tbsp of sugar
>
> small bunch of mint
>
> soda water (sparkling water will do too)
>
> 3 limes, juiced

Method

Step 1: *Mash the sugar and mint leaves together using a pestle and mortar. If you don't have one, just tear the leaves and use the back of a spoon to crush the sugar.*

Step 2: *Grab two glasses and put a handful of ice into each one. Evenly divide the lime juice between them and add the mint and sugar mix. Top up with soda water, add a straw and serve.*

Speaking of nights out, half the craic is the getting ready ...

I LOVE THE TASTE OF CHOCOLATE SO MUCH (GOD, I REALLY LOVE CHOCOLATE) BUT I CAN'T HAVE IT ALL THE TIME.

What we know now about

hair

OR, WHY YOU'LL NEVER HAVE POCAHONTAS HAIR AND THAT'S OK

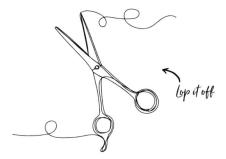

lop it off

The wonder of a good haircut

J How come every time you see a famous person they always have long, swishy, shiny, luxurious hair? Do they all have fantastic hair genes or are they all wearing wigs? I am someone who is not blessed with 'good' hair. It wasn't always that way — I blame my children. My hair started falling out big time after I had my first child. I had that weird, sticky-up hair at the front that had to be flattened down with hairspray if I was going out. But I really noticed it after I had my second child. The very annoying thing is, when you are pregnant, your hair plays a trick on you and it looks great. I'm serious! The next time you see a pregnant woman pay attention to her hair — I bet it will look thick, shiny and glossy. It's all those hormones pumping around her body. But of course, things change, and once that baby comes out then your hair starts falling out! Not in clumps (please don't panic if you are reading this while pregnant with your first child) but you will definitely notice it — oh hello, sticky-up hair bits in the front, oh look at my non-existent ponytail. I knew there were only two options here — to freak out and travel to Turkey ASAP for a hair transplant or to embrace my new lack of hirsuteness and ignore it. And, dear reader, that would have worked, except for the fact that I know Mairéad Ronan. She of the swishy Pocahontas hair.

If you are like me, you might be surprised to hear that there are masks for your hair — yes really! Like a mask for your face except for your hair. I had pooh-poohed that until I was told categorically that they do work, they will help heal your hair follicles (are you now, like me, imagining a spiritual hair guru with his hands on your head?) and they will do wonders for the overall look of your hair. That and a good haircut.

And no, that does not mean putting a towel around your neck and telling your husband to 'just lop it off' (this did actually happen during lockdown in 2021). There is something nerve-racking about walking into a hair salon, particularly a good one with cool-looking hairdressers all strutting around in their cool clothes and hair — I suddenly become inarticulate when asked what I'm looking to have done and end up holding out my phone, showing a picture of a model with lovely, thick, luscious hair, grunting, 'This.' Or worse, I smile sweetly and say, 'Whatever you think yourself' — THIS IS NOT A GOOD IDEA. As amazing as this hairdresser could be, they do not know you and do not know your style. They might read you completely wrong and give you a 'do' and before you know it you are thanking her, tipping her way over the odds and bowing as you exit the hair salon with a sensible haircut that you are going to cry over for the next few weeks. Or maybe that's just me.

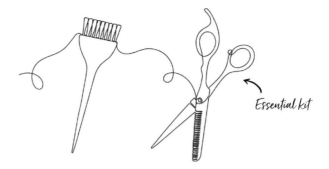

Essential kit

There is no silver lining to getting grey hair ...

M August 2001 — there it was. I kept pulling and tugging at it, trying to see if the colourist had made a mistake, because a small section of my roots were grey ... well, actually, more white. Over the next few weeks more and more of them appeared. I was only 21; how the hell was this happening to me? My much older sisters had NO grey hairs and they were in their 30s, which to me meant they were probably alive when the dinosaurs were roaming the earth. In the previous five months I'd lost my mother to cancer, I'd lost my tonsils, I'd lost my confidence and now I was losing my natural mousey–brown hair colour (which I'd never loved anyway). From the age of 16 I had been messing with my hair, from ironing it with an actual iron before going to the No Name Disco, to my first set of highlights (which was VERY traumatic. It involved a cap that looked like a swimming hat but with tiny holes all over it. The stylist was gowned up like a surgeon and came at me with what looked like a crochet needle and began to roughly pull my hair through the tiny holes in said swimming cap). But now, with these grey hairs, I would have to continue to be a salon regular whether I wanted to or not.

At the time I loved wearing my hair in a middle parting, so I could already see that this was going to be a lifelong, expensive secret. But thank the gods that are Peter Mark, because their staff have been tinting and masking my hair every month ever since. And over all those visits I've calculated that I've spent approximately €28,000 on masking my grey hair (roughly €100 per month x 12 = €1,200 then multiply that by 23 years ... shocking!). Hair is BIG business! And in a way, that's how I ended up starting a hairbrush business ...

There's a misconception that when you work in telly you have a professional hair and make-up team with you at all times. But this depends on the show and only the bigger budget programmes would have this kind of set-up. So most Irish TV presenters will do their own hair and make-up. For years, working on shows like *Celebrity Bainisteoir*, a travel show called *Getaways* and about seven years of *Ireland's Fittest Family*, I did my own hair and make-up. It worked because we were always outdoors in all sorts of weather and so in a way I needed to look as windswept as the families ... I think I achieved this quite well. I remember watching an episode that we had filmed in Connemara at the beginning of a storm. As I said my closing piece to camera, I looked as though I'd been crying because my mascara was under my eyes, over my eyes and on my cheeks, and the cameraman never mentioned it. And my hair wasn't much better.

But it was on these shoots when I would have to fix my hair yet again after a lot of rain or crazy gusts of wind that I had the idea to create a brilliant blow-drying brush. I knew what handle it should have, what type of bristles, the size it needed to be and it also needed a heat protection cap at the top. I kept the idea (like most women do) in my head for over a year, maybe longer, because I didn't have the confidence to do anything about it. But one morning when the Coronas were on *The Ray D'Arcy Show* in Today FM, I was chatting to their manager. He just dropped into the conversation that his sister was manufacturing make-up brushes, and would I try them out and give her some feedback? I did and they were excellent quality. That was my 'PING A-HA' moment. Maybe this girl, Debbie, could help me get my idea out of my head and into production? We arranged to meet in a café in Dublin 2 and it was kind of like an awkward first date. I talked her through what I wanted to create, and she took my fairly wrecked-looking hairbrushes away. I remember thinking, 'I wish I'd cleaned them a bit more,' because there were strands of my hair wrapped around them. But that coffee was the day that FARO Beauty was born. We decided to go into business together. After a number of years we decided to grow the team from two to three. Aoife, our social media, website and marketing manager, gave the brand new life. I'm really proud of what Debbie, Aoife and I achieved. We're still going, but it hasn't always been easy.

The funny thing is, with all the hair hang-ups I have with hiding my grey, I've had so many compliments about my hair over the years and was even hired as the face (or head) of a campaign with Garnier — I was the perfect candidate because I could prove that their hair colour did in fact cover stubborn greys.

So, I've been auburn, auburn with honey highlights, copper, copper with balayage, rich brown, frosted chestnut (which was almost black!) and everything in between ... but I'm now a blonde. And because of that, I gain a whole two extra weeks on my roots, which is better for my hair, better for my pocket and I've way more news to give my hair stylist.

EVEN
WITH THAT
GREAT NEW
HAIRDRESSER,
IT'S IMPORTANT
TO BE
REALISTIC
ABOUT WHAT
MIRACLES THEY
CAN PERFORM.

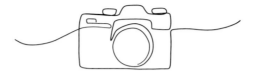

Mairéad's top tips for camera-ready hair

I'm aware that most people don't have to worry about going live on TV day-to-day, but if you've ever wondered how influencers manage to look so groomed in those oh-so-casual at-home shots, here's what I've learned about looking a bit more composed from my many hair fails over the years:

Invest in a good brush (#NOTANAD, I'm just telling you about FARO) Our brushes are ceramic coated, which means the entire barrel of the brush heats up quickly and evenly. This reduces the amount of time your hair is exposed to heat from the hairdryer, resulting in less heat damage. Ceramic hairbrushes also eliminate static electricity, which causes flyaways and frizz. Most importantly, they are very affordable — and will last.

So here's the cheeky plug: I recommend the Faro 32mm as the best blow-drying brush, because it's suitable for all lengths from bob to long hair and will give you a gorgeous blow-dry in minutes.

Spend as much as you can on shampoo My favourite is L'Oréal Professionnel Metal Detox shampoo. I know salon shampoos are more expensive, but you use a lot less and you will notice a difference a huge difference within weeks. Jenny was using shower gels at one point ... I KNOW, bonkers! But I've convinced her to change her ways and she now agrees with me on this one. The best description I've heard is that shampoos are like olive oils — you can get one for €4, but the one that costs €14 is a million times better for you, and tastes better, too.

And if you have thinning hair Try Nioxin cleansing shampoo. Their entire range is excellent if you have thinning hair. Ask your salon which one would be best for you. (But also see your doctor if this persists.)

Use a hair mask once a week My favourite is L'Oréal Professionnel Metal Detox mask – I have instantly smoother, shinier hair after using this. It also protects hair from breakage. It's really lightweight too, so your hair won't feel gloopy or greasy after using. But remember, when using a mask, apply from mid length to ends only and less is more.

Invest in your hairdryer I recommend the ETI Line Plus digital hairdryer. It's very lightweight and costs €115 (approximately).

I've tried SO many hairdryers over the years, even the very expensive ones (cough, cough, Dyson), but this is hands–down the best.

For best results, blast dry your hair until it's about 70 per cent dry before you start to style it, then dry your hair in sections. Never place the dryer directly on the hair – keep it about 10 or 12 cm away and keep the brush turning as you dry.

Did you know that hairdryers need to be changed every two years? After two years they can start to overheat and cause damage to your hair. This one is a brilliant tool and costs €57.50 per year of use – that's really good value.

And if you're going 'Out Out' …

Invest in some easy hair tools to make the extra effort I love the Hot Tools Gold Curl Bar, 25mm size – the easiest way to create soft, beachy waves in minutes. You cannot make a mistake with this one because it's shaped like a hairdryer and the angle means it's much easier for the non–professionals (most of us) to use. But be careful, it gets really hot. Make sure to always use the heat protection mat that comes with it when placing it back down on a surface.

How to pick your hairdresser

J If you have a friend with a great hairdo, get a recommendation from her (or, in my case, ask Mairéad). But even with that great new hairdresser, it's important to be realistic about what miracles they can perform. Arriving in with a picture of Jennifer Aniston will not make you turn into Jennifer Aniston. If you are the type of person who doesn't blow–dry her hair then you need to be honest with your hairdresser and tell her this. There is no point getting a do that needs daily fixing if you can't even manage a blow–dry. Same goes for the cut — make sure it's one you can manage. We are all time–poor and the less faffing around we have to do in the morning, the better. And my last bit of advice here — if you hate your haircut then tell your hairdresser. There is nothing worse than smiling through gritted teeth and then getting home and crying into the mirror and refusing to leave your house for two weeks. If you let your hairdresser know you are unhappy then maybe (fingers crossed) she can do something about it. I am fully aware that you would rather eat your own shoe than complain, but it's for the best, trust me.

Tips for styling your hair

- I have learned to use heat protective spray – have I left it too late? Probably, but I use it religiously now. Spray it on towel-dried hair before blow-drying. I use a few different ones:

- Scrimpy – got2b Guardian Angel (available from Boots, €6.49)

- Spendy – Kérastase Nutritive Nectar Thermique (guide price €36)

- Make sure you get yourself a great blow-dry brush (see Mairéad's advice above)

Hair products and accessories

Redken Acidic Bonding Concentrate shampoo and conditioner
This product range helps restore damaged hair. I was sceptical before I tried it, but this stuff has helped my hair and it needed help!

Dry shampoo – a magic product for fine hair Because I have such fine hair (probably not helped by the fact that I used to wash it every single day) dry shampoo is a godsend. A little bit of this goes a long way and now I can go three days between washes. Three days! This has been a game changer and a time saver. No more faffing around with hairdryers and brushes, just a quick light spray at the roots, comb through and my hair looks thicker and, because I'm not washing it so often, it is looking so much better. I use Batiste Original Dry Shampoo, but there are loads out there so try a few before you settle on the one best suited for you.

My favourite is Klorane, a French brand that's found in many pharmacies. Ⓜ

Hair extensions

I've had hair extensions put in a few times over the years. It's an amazing feeling to go from having a small little ponytail to actually something to grab on to. It increased my confidence – which is nuts, as I don't know if anyone actually noticed except me. But each time I got them in, after a short while I began dreaming of getting them taken out again. You do feel them, and they do catch when you brush your hair. And when they are growing out, they can really begin to annoy you. Of course, if you don't want to commit 100 per cent you can get clip-ins, which are great for a night out. The clip-ins that I have used in the past were from Hairspray – they have salons all over the country.

Either way, there are lots of options nowadays to help when you're having a bad hair day – and if you don't fancy any of them, there are always hats!

If you are considering hair extensions, go speak to the professionals.

'I need a change ... I'll cut my hair off'

We've all been there. I mean they've even written a bloody song about it – 'I'm gonna wash that man right outta my hair' – or, in some cases, cut it all off as a symbol of FREEDOM. Usually I'm all on for acts of spontaneity, but STOP RIGHT THERE. Do you really think it's a good idea to cut all your hair off just because you've finally broken free of a bad relationship? Maybe take a pause, a breather, a looong walk with a friend and hold off on making that decision. There are lots of apps out there now where you can put different haircuts on your gorgeous face to see what suits you before you go into the hairdresser shouting, 'I NEED A CHANGE NOWWW – CUT IT ALL OFF.' Just make sure you have really thought about the cut because you do not want to be sad about a break-up (even one that you instigated) and sad about a bad hairdo at the same time. This could send you over the emotional edge. And we do not want that.

'Women over a certain age need to cut that hair and get a "do"'

Is it here that I mention the age thing? That time in a woman's life when she chops off her hair because she feels too old for long hair. Sure, only young wans are allowed to have long, flowy hair. Or is that a load of bollox we have been fed over the years, by whom I'm not sure – The Media? Men? Our mothers? Either way, I'm here to say that if you want to keep your Pocahontas-long hair till you are 90 then do it; do not be swayed by what you 'think' you should do because society tells you to. And the other side of the coin is, if you want a short pixie cut, then do that too. Don't be told what a woman should look like. Just look like yourself, whatever age you are. Because, as Dr Seuss says, 'There is no one alive that is youer than you!'

To grey or not to grey?

There is a whole cohort of women out there who are ditching the hair dye and going for the all-grey look. Personally, I think it looks fantastic. There is something about a woman reclaiming her right to do whatever she wants and look however she likes that is so sexy. Grey hair used to signal OLD and a sense of giving up. Not anymore. My grey is not in yet, so I don't have to make that choice, but something tells me I'll be in the land of grey as soon as it starts to happen.

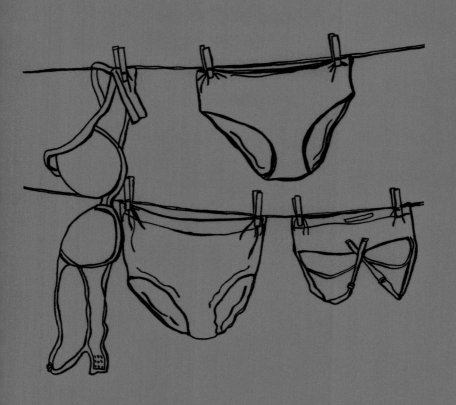

What we know now about

fashion

OR, WHY YOU NEED TO SPEND MONEY WHERE YOU SPEND YOUR TIME

Women who wear black lead colourful lives

I love black clothes. What is not to like? They look stylish and cool with minimal effort. Mairéad gives out to me for wearing too much black, but I love it. I go mad sometimes and wear stripes and there have been times when I have gone utterly mad and worn a colour. I initially like it but then I'm secretly dreaming of putting on some black as soon as I can. There is something about black that says: my clothes are not talking for me. They are a blank slate to my personality. They are chic and classic with a hint of 'not trying too hard'. My other fave colours to wear are navy, grey, oatmeal and white. All beautiful and so easy to wear. I love the stories you hear about very famous people and entrepreneurs who have minimised their wardrobe down to multiple versions of the same black/grey outfit. Think Steve Jobs, Angelina Jolie, Audrey Hepburn or Tom Ford (and Hillary Clinton and her famous pantsuits!).

I am so happy I am living though this fashion era where athleisure wear is a thing. Where dressing down is the new dressing up. Birkenstocks and jeans, a cosy fleece and a pair of leggings, baggy trousers and a sweatshirt, oversized shirt and jeans ... all of these combinations are winners in my eyes. I am not a fan of dressing up. I know that for a lot of women this is a joy. Getting out of the normal day-to-day gear and getting all dollied up and fancy is their idea of bliss. Not for me. It's a pain. Uncomfortable underwear and too-tight clothing is my nightmare scenario. I don't feel myself. I feel like I am in fancy dress.

I do remember one night out in particular with Mairéad where I felt a million dollars. We were going to the Style Awards, and I had prepped to within an inch of my life. Our friend Yvonne Maher, who is a magician when it comes to make-up, did both of ours. I rented a

Rixo dress from Happy Days dress rental shop and I was moisturised and buffed. When I looked in the mirror, I did not recognise myself. I looked fantastic. I was admiring myself as if I were looking at someone else. 'Wow,' I thought, 'She looks hot.' But Jesus Christ, the effort! I could not be arsed. It takes so much time to look great. Hair appointments, nails, tan, make-up application, shopping for 'the dress' ... all of these eat into time, time where I could be reading a book or going for a walk with my dogs or just having a cup of tea in the garden. So, once a year maybe, I can do it (every two years, maybe!) because it was fun to play dress-up and to look like that, but I'd take jeans, a jumper and a pair of runners any day.

Big bust and top heavy

My shape is top heavy. Big bust and a bit of a belly. My style is casual. I love jeans, jumpers, shirts, runners, boots and coats and trouser suits. In the summer I live in shorts, shirts and Birkenstocks.

I stopped wearing high heels years ago — life is too short to mash your feet into something so painful. And for what? To elongate the leg? Nah, my legs are the way they are, thank you very much (I have however worn a kitten heel occasionally — not too painful and something pointy can look cute with a dress).

I have days where I live in a pair of Lululemons (expensive but worth it), t-shirt and jumper, and other days where I make more of an effort and go with a nice top and jeans. It's the same for hair and make-up. Some days I lash the make-up on because maybe I feel tired and drab, and other days I like the freshness of a light base and nothing much else. But I will always wear a light foundation base. It's like putting on clean knickers every day; it has to be done.

My fashion like list

I like big knickers After two C-sections, these are a must — begone bikini knickers or thongs — and as for those short-type ones, just no. Marks and Spencer are always my go-to choice. They call the style Full Briefs. Cotton and comfy.

I like bras with an underwire So I can hoosh my boobs up with a tightening of a strap. It is worth it to go to a proper underwear shop. There is one such shop in Stillorgan in County Dublin called Contour. You know you are in safe bra hands when you go in here. Marks and Spencer also offer a great bra measuring service. I read not so long ago that up to 80 per cent of us are wearing the wrong size bra! It's amazing what a good, proper fitting bra can do for your posture and your size. It changes how you look in a top. I have tried those Spandex-type bras — the ones that are supposed to fit you like a second skin — and they do absolutely nothing for me. I like the idea of them but the reality is flat boobs and squishy back. Not a good look in my opinion.

I like vests My vest of choice is called the Cool Comfort from Marks and Spencer — the tag line is that it keeps you feeling fresh all day. I agree. I couldn't wear a t-shirt or top without one of these on — it makes everything feel nice and secure. I've never tried Skims, which some people swear by, so maybe I'll put these on my birthday list.

I like jeans that are high-waisted Mom jeans, yes, skinny jeans, no. I'm in a lot of like with high-waisted flared jeans at the moment. I like the feel of them with a jumper and a long coat or coatigan (worst word in fashion but descriptive). I have a gorgeous pair of Levi's High Rise Ribcage that I love. Salsa jeans are so comfy and give you great shape, and of course Marks and Spencer do lots of affordable different shapes and lengths to suit everyone.

I like jumpers Especially spendy cashmere ones from Marks and Spencer – I buy one a year (OK, maybe two) and wear them to death. They are so soft and feel amazing on. Carolyn Donnelly in Dunnes do beautiful cashmere–blend jumpers that are so soft and wash very well.

I like shirts All sorts – stripy or plain, oversized or fitted. You can't go wrong with a shirt.

I like blazer-style jackets They give structure and I think they look really flattering. The last trouser suit I bought was from Jaeger in Marks and Spencer. It's one that I'll be able to swap up with different outfits so worth the money, I think.

I like minimal jewellery I used to be all silver but I think gold is warmer on my skin now. I wear my engagement ring every day and then swap around the rest, with different versions of gold necklaces and gold hoop earrings or a pair of small diamond earrings. Either way, it's minimal. I am not a fan of chunky jewellery and yet love everything Prue Leith wears on *Great British Bake Off*! I will definitely be one of those women who wear huge colourful glasses as I age – like Iris Apfel, the American fashion designer and icon who died in 2024 at the age of 102. Now, *she* was fabulous.

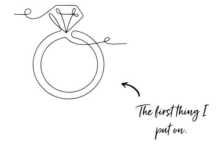

The first thing I put on.

'Trendy is the last stage before tacky'

KARL LAGERFELD

M I was always a slave to trendy clothes in my youth which, according to Karl, is a very bad thing. But at the age of 36, after I had Eliza, I completely lost my way around my wardrobe. I suppose spending six months wearing breastfeeding tops every day will do that to you. Any time I look at photos from that year I think, 'What the hell are you wearing?' I somehow went from being someone who knew what to wear most of the time to full-on hicky hickster. I was *trying* to introduce 'trends' after the pregnancy, but nothing looked right. And so, I continued to buy more clothes, always repeating the same mistakes. In the end I had a bulging wardrobe full of clothes that did nothing for me. So I decided to do something I had never done before ...

Hiring a stylist

Yes, I'd worked with lots of stylists on magazine shoots and telly projects, but this was different. I now needed someone to come to my home, go through my wardrobe and dress me, because I had lost the ability to do so myself. I used 'Style Savvy' – a.k.a. Laura Jordan. She was (and still is) brilliant. Laura asked me to talk through an average week, because my wardrobe needed to reflect what I was actually doing. So, armed with that info, she then went through my wardrobe.

It turns out I had a lot of going-out clothes, but I was going nowhere other than my son's GAA matches. And I was wearing Eliza in a sling every day. We kept the few items I was using and then she emailed me a list with links to things to buy. By the end of the process, I had a wardrobe that had a lot less in it, yet I had far more outfits to choose from each day. It's a kind of wardrobe sorcery.

If you are having a wardrobe wobble like I was, then this is a really good thing to do. It might sound a little excessive but it was really affordable and ultimately stopped me wasting more money buying things that didn't work. Many of the bigger department stores will also often offer a version of this service for free (like Brown Thomas and Arnotts).

The best way to be sustainable with your clothes is to buy less

According to *Vogue* (and they know) a 'sufficient' wardrobe consists of 74 garments, which is 20 outfits in total. This is broken down into:

- 6 outfits for work
- 3 outfits for home wear/day wear
- 3 outfits for sports/the gym
- 2 outfits for occasions
- 4 outdoor jackets
- With the remaining two outfits coming from a mix of trousers/skirts and tops.

What they don't have on that list is a funeral outfit. Everyone needs one of these because, let's face it, you don't get much notice.

Make it work

Put your money where you spend your time

This is the best piece of advice when it comes to buying clothing. We have all been guilty of buying a dress for a Christmas party or wedding and not blinking at the price of it, but only wearing it that one time. This doesn't make a lick of sense. When it comes to clothes, put your money where you spend your time.

If most of your time is spent working, invest in really good workwear. If you live in leggings and sweatshirts, buy good-quality ones. Don't think of it as a waste to spend a bit more on these items.

Make time to save time

I like a uniform — not to the same extent as Geri Halliwell-Horner (she only wears white), but I do wear roughly the same 15 items of clothing each week. Think about what you have worn over the last week and you'll probably agree.

So, when I have a busy week coming up, I will make a wardrobe plan, which is exactly the same as a meal plan but with clothes. Write down the day of the week and what you will wear on each day. For women who have to wear business attire it's a good idea to buy a small clothes rail and get your outfits ready for the week.

Shapewear... or, as we call it, sucky-in stuff

The pants that promise to sculpt, control, flatten, cinch and smooth. And they do — if you buy the right size. Unfortunately, if you get a size too small you will find yourself in a toilet cubicle sweating while trying to peel them off and throw them in a bin. So, when shopping for sucky-in stuff, always try on. We all know different brands = different sizes = different fits! Getting the right size will also stop them rolling at the top.

Bras – always wear a new bra on the loosest hook

A mistake I made for years was, when trying on a bra, I would have it on the tightest clasp. But washing and wearing it would make it looser and I would lose support! So, always wear a new bra on the loosest hook and eye, then over time as it stretches out, move it to the middle and finally the tightest one (and after that, chuck it).

Sports bras

Back when Jenny and I were on radio together, this was one of the most-asked questions: what is the BEST sports bra out there? Irish women have big chests and it's not fun to run with your boobs flapping all over the place.

We tried and tested so many bras and at the time the Enell was the best one. It was designed by a big-busted volleyball player who had to wear two sports bras to feel any sort of support and it's available in size C upwards. Now I have the Shock Absorber Infinity power bra. It's front-closing and holds the girls in place while doing cardio ... highly recommended.

'**Clothes aren't going to change the world.**

The women who wear them are.

ANNE KLEIN

What we know now about

cleaning

OR, WHY
CLEANING
IS *(nearly)*
BETTER
THAN SEX

Zen and the art of cleaning

J Feeling slightly high, a bit sweaty and have a smile of satisfaction on your face? You must have just given the house a good clean! We both love nothing better than a clean. We can sit down together with a pot of tea and bore the knickers off each other about the cleaning we have both done in our respective homes. We discuss cleaning hacks we have tried out and products we have bought and acknowledge how happy it makes both of us feel. We've said it again and again on the podcast, cleaning can be a form of meditation and it is oh so satisfying. If you want to change your life, our advice is to start with a good house scrub.

(In fact, instead of writing this book, I have just vacuumed the whole house, followed by a quick bathroom and toilet clean and ending with a whole-house floor steam clean.)

I love a good clean. I love the physicality of it. Sometimes when I know it's going to be a full top-to-bottom house clean, I'll put my headphones in and pop on an audiobook or podcast and happily work away for a few hours. Other times, I just want the noise of the clean, nothing else — and, boy, the satisfaction. I've watched old movies of cowboys leaning back on a fence after making sure their animals are safe and sound after being rounded up — well, that's me after I've folded a pile of washing, washed and steam-cleaned the floors and scrubbed the toilets. If I smoked, I'd have one.

I can often be found sitting on the couch looking intently at my phone, watching someone else clean their shower/bath/windows/floors. My favourite noise? When the dishwasher is running. So soothing.

Cleaning products I couldn't do without

The Addis Mop As I've already mentioned, the other noise I love is the *tsss, tsss* of my spray mop. I have moved onto my latest one, the Addis, and it feels like the Rolls Royce of spray mops. If you don't have one, you need one! I'm not exaggerating when I say it will make your life easier and you will feel deep, deep love for it and what it does. It's a mop that has a refillable bottle attached that allows you to mop without the hassle of filling a bucket. You simply fill the bottle with your floor cleaner and some lukewarm water and off you go with your trigger handle making the *tsss, tsss* noise, spraying water onto the floor in front of the mop. It's fast, efficient and oh so handy, especially if you have pets and/or children. I love mine so much I just leave it sitting out all day by my kitchen island. It's like an art installation of love, an ode to cleaning. One of those cleaning products I just wouldn't do without.

The many miracles of white vinegar Another cleaning product I use that is not expensive and works wonders on nearly everything in your home is white vinegar. I remember sharing this cleaning hack on the podcast: it was something I saw online and could not believe how brilliantly it worked when I tried it.

The Dishmatic scrubbing brush That's the scrubbing brush with the sponge on the end. You can screw off the top and pour in washing-up liquid for washing the dishes, BUT if you fill it halfway with white vinegar and top it off with the washing liquid, it is the best cleaner of EVERYTHING. Use it on your taps, your shower doors, your sink, your door handles, your children (that is a joke) … things come up SPARKLING! It is magic.

I took a break to clean my washing machine

BIT OF A BREAK You wouldn't have noticed, but I just stopped writing there for five minutes because I wanted to clean my washing machine. A great hack is to pour two cups of white vinegar into the detergent dispenser. Run it on a hot cycle and TA–DA. The same goes for your dishwasher – except in that case, pour white vinegar into a cup and leave it in the top shelf of the dishwasher as you run a cycle. Another TA–DA!

It's the simple things that keep me happy the longer I'm on the planet. And a clean house is one of those things.

The Karcher SC3 Steam cleaner It's a bit pricey but so worth it in my opinion. After you've used it, you feel like professional cleaners have been in – your home feels squeaky clean. You can use it everywhere. It's brilliant on mouldy grout in the shower and so good on floors. I've used it to clean my kitchen cabinets, cooker hob, the loos ... it works wonders and is a great investment.

Miele C3 Complete Dog and Cat If you have animals, then my top recommendation is the Miele C3 Complete Dog and Cat. I've tried the very well-known cordless one, but I ended up going back to this. In my opinion, it's the best. Yes, it's more expensive than other brands, but it's never let me down.

Mairead's can't-live-without cleaning tips and hero products

M And here is my list of must-haves to ensure (almost) domestic bliss.

Best vacuum – this one is tricky because I have two (I know, I know!)

- Dyson Cordless V15 Detect

- Miele Complete C3 Parquet XL. It has the greatest suction and almost lifts the carpet up, but it's a plug-in one, so you have to stop and move around to different sockets

Rinse hose When installing showers or baths, ALWAYS make sure to include a rinse hose. It's impossible to clean without them.

Under-the-sink essentials

- Cif cream cleaner – the original and best for cleaning sinks and anything greasy

- Pink Stuff paste – is there anything this can't clean? Glass, BBQs, garden furniture, pots and pans, tiles … the list goes on. BUT always try on a small, not visible area first and never on anything that's still hot.

Cleaning jobs I hate

Not all cleaning jobs are equal. Some I would happily leave to others.

Changing bed sheets My tip for motivating yourself to get this done is to visualise that delicious feeling when you crawl into bed at the end of a long day. I let out a long sigh and think to myself that this must be what heaven feels like. The practical job of getting the sheets, duvet covers and pillowcases off, into the wash and then back on again is torture. But we have to be thankful for the invention of duvets.

Ironing is another hate job I don't iron a thing. Nothing. If it needs to be ironed, you're doing it yourself. I have a husband who is an excellent ironer — so that job goes to him (alternatively, you can always just pop things that are nearly dry in the dryer for 10 minutes, shake out and fold while still warm to get the wrinkles out.)

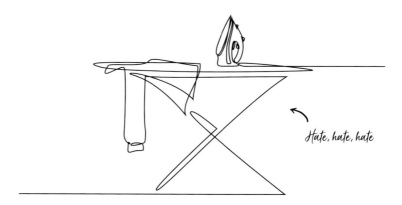

Hate, hate, hate

But how do you keep on top of all the cleaning all the time?

J A basic rule I have that keeps our home running smoothly and makes sure that things don't build up (and I'm not left with a massive cleaning job to do at the weekend) is to tip away every day. I'm always picking up clothes and shoes and putting them back in rooms. I won't go to bed unless the kitchen is clean and set up for the next morning, and the same goes for the TV room — I make sure that all cushions are put back and throws folded. Same goes for when I get up in the morning — the first thing I do is make our bed. It's a way for me to start the day positively — and you might think, 'How does feckin' making your bed do that?', but there is something about a job done first thing that allows me to face the rest of the day head-on.

I need to stress here that I'm not a clean freak — not like a neighbour of ours whose house I went into when I was around eleven years old. She had the plastic still on the couch! I am not lying. I remember going into the sitting room and hearing the crunch of the plastic on the couch when I sat down. Although, in saying that, I have sometimes wanted to wrap Stanley the Golden Retriever up in plastic to stop him shedding everywhere in our house!

Cleaning and tidying are NOT the same thing!

M I love cleaning ... give me a set of Marigold gloves (size small, preferably yellow) and I'm happy out. I get giddy at the thoughts of an empty house and getting stuck into a deep clean. When I am in that zone it is the only time that my mind is calm. So as I'm scrubbing or mopping, I'm somehow rinsing my brain, decluttering my mind and becoming relaxed. It doesn't make sense, but at times I've felt more relaxed doing this than I am in a spa getting a back massage.

I have tried journalling but all I end up with is a to-do list, which makes me feel more anxious. I have tried guided meditation, but end up feeling silly and embarrassed. And I have tried yoga, but each course I sign up to I find myself surrounded by beautiful, bendy women and then I become tense and intimidated.

But when I clean, I feel like I get to the same place that all of these things are trying to achieve. A state of quiet, relaxed calm and when I'm finished ... satisfaction.

A huge number of arguments at home are caused by who does which cleaning jobs and when and how well they do them. But most of my *cleaning time* is taken up by *tidying*, or to give it its full title: PUTTING EVERYONE ELSE'S CRAP AWAY!

Which brings me nicely along to ...

We ALL have too much stuff It's true, all of us, even you, the person reading this. You've too many black tops, too many t-shirts, too many pairs of black leggings, jeans, knickers, bras and socks, sets of PJs, too many towels and tea towels, too many notebooks, pens, chargers, mugs, pots, pans, toys (oh, the toys), art supplies and too much just-in-case stuff. Most people assume that they just need to become more organised but the truth is, if you are trying to manage too much stuff, you'll fail.

It's the drowning in stuff that makes cleaning so overwhelming for many. Recently a friend of mine told me that she wished they could move house because their three-bed semi-D is 'too small'. I told her that she doesn't need more space, she needs LESS stuff (when I type in caps, it means I'm shouting ... sorry).

When I was growing up everyone's house was very clean and tidy. The reason wasn't because they were all trying to win Housewife of the Year. It was because we had less stuff.

I never remember feeling like I didn't have enough of anything — because I had enough of everything. I had enough clothes, enough food, enough toys, enough books ... but not too much of anything.

Go and do a big dump! Decluttering your home will make it more peaceful and SO EASY to clean. Start small — some kitchen drawers today or your knicker drawer or under the sink tomorrow.

The following process will help you no matter what area you are clearing:

Create three piles:

- **Keep:** Obviously, keep the items you use or wear regularly.

- **Dump:** No discussion necessary: if you have not worn an item in over a year, move it along. Same rule applies to your kitchen. You do not need 26 mugs.

- **Maybe/mend:** This pile might be something you like but the zip is broken or it's missing a button. It could also be a sentimental item of clothing or a tea set from Granny. This is the one that needs a bit of time.

After you've done this, put all the 'keep' pieces back in the wardrobe/hotpress/cupboard, bag the 'dump' items correctly and either give them away to a charity or the clothes bank.

This is IMPORTANT: after the big dump, do NOT go out and re-stuff the drawers, wardrobes and cabinets again with new things!

Clean your home like you're a professional who has been hired for one hour This was great advice I got when I moved out of home for the first time. It stopped me procrastinating for ever about cleaning a room. At the end of that hour, down tools and do no more.

Remember your home is not a show house so it doesn't have to look like one Mess happens. It's OK.

Marigolds + Mop = Calmness

CLEAN
YOUR HOME
LIKE
YOU'RE A
PROFESSIONAL
WHO HAS
BEEN HIRED
FOR ONE
HOUR.

What we know now about

dinner

OR, THE RELENTLESS HELL OF COMING UP WITH DINNERS FOR THE REST OF YOUR LIFE

Whoever invented dinners can just get in the sea

J No one tells you when you are younger that you are going to spend years of your life being asked one question or asking yourself one question – 'What's for dinner?' It's relentless. You see, the thing is, just when you've made dinner and cleaned up, you are thinking about tomorrow's dinner and whether you have the ingredients for it or if you'll have to go to the supermarket for the tenth time that day. It says more about me that I am friendlier with the people who work in my local SuperValu than people I've known all my life. I was worried one day and asked Gillian on the cash desk whether I was the person who was in the supermarket the most out of everyone who came in. She leaned in towards me and whispered, 'You're not the worst.' That, to me, was not a positive. I wasn't the best either.

Anyway, to get back to dinners – whoever invented them can just get in the sea. Us women would be fine having the odd dinner of a bag of popcorn or toast and a scrambled egg, or my favourite, the picky–picky dinner – basically anything you can throw onto a plate with some crackers and eat. But the reality is, if you are cooking for others or want to at least try and meet your basic daily nutritional requirements, a little more effort is required.

Love is in the air (fryer!)

I am in love with my air fryer. It has made my life easier and because of that, I give thanks. Here is possibly a bit of hyperbole, but see if you agree. I'll put it in caps to make it even more dramatic: THE INVENTION OF THE AIR FRYER IS EQUIVALENT TO THE INVENTION OF THE MOBILE PHONE. That is an actual statement

I made one evening to my husband after making some nice crispy cubed potatoes. They were delicious and so quick and easy and the cleaning, sure well, that was done before I knew it. I find myself standing over my air fryer, looking quizzically at it, mumbling, 'How does it not have to be heated up?' I don't understand how it works and I don't care. It has changed my life. Dinners are now not as horrific as they used to be.

If you are still on the fence about buying one, I AM SHOUTING AT YOU NOW TO GET OFF THAT FENCE AND GET ONE. We have the Ninja Dual Zone Air Fryer and I use it every day and only turn on my oven for pizza-making or the grill at the weekend.

There are so many Instagram accounts and books out now with air fryer recipes that there are no end of ideas, but some of my favourites are: cubed potatoes, caprese chicken, sausage rolls, stuffed chicken and bacon, bang bang chicken (chicken goujons), breaded fish, chicken melts ... and on and on.

The other thing that has helped make dinners easier is Instagram. There are so many accounts to choose from and so many helpful dinner ideas that when I am at a loss about what to make (which is a lot of the time), I can just go online and find something. Some of my favourites are:

- @nevenmaguire
- @thebatchlady
- @boredoflunch
- @liliforberg
- @littleloucooks
- @lilly_higgins_

Just eat the vegetables!

There's no shame in accommodating picky eaters. What is rarely spoken about in most family households is the whole rigmarole of having to cook a few different dinners because you are surrounded by choosy individuals. This is nearly as shameful as 'my children won't eat vegetables'. When I was young and still being handed my dinner (oh, to go back to those days), I would turn up my nose at stews (ewww, wet potatoes), liver (just, no), omelettes (runny eggs and vegetables – I rest my case) and anything that involved the very scary pressure cooker. Yet now I eat all of the above (except liver because that's just gross). So, the multiple dinners I end up cooking I resign myself to. It won't last forever and there will come a day when we won't all be together and I'll be crying into my husband's face about the heady days of multiple dinner makings (or maybe not ...).

My lotto dinner dream

I love the 'What would you do if you won the lotto?' game. The funny thing is, if you went by the TV ads you'd think we'd all be building water slides in our back gardens. The truth is for most women the first thing we'd do is employ a full-time chef. Imagine! It would be like living with the Kardashians without having to live with them – you could stroll up to your kitchen counter and request a salad or a sandwich without batting an eyelid. No more would the question of 'What are we having for dinner?' reverberate around the house – the chef would be standing by with their weekly dinner plan, spooning it all out on demand. One can dream.

Husband is really the cook in this house but he has to put up with my mediocre cooking until he either decides to become a stay-at-home parent or retire. Actually, hang on ... I've just realised as I type this that I will one day have my very own private chef. His name is Ray!

I actually like cooking ... it's just **having** *to do it!*

After all that ranting, the odd fact is that I quite like cooking ... but not all the time. And that's the issue — it's the HAVING to do it. I like nothing better some days than chopping up lots of vegetables and making a stir fry or a soup, I make a mean Marry Me chicken (@boredoflunch), I love salmon (even though Mairéad has tried to turn me off it) and I love making my 'Jenny Kelly Salad' (think 1980s salad with a few fancy things thrown into the mix — and see the recipe below). And I enjoy a bit of baking too — like banana bread (@donalskehan) or chocolate biscuit cake (@odlums_ireland) and I love to make good old-fashioned buns (www.bbcgoodfood.com).

Jenny Kelly Salad (aka 1980s salad)

1/2 cucumber, chopped

Large tomato, chopped

2 tbsp spicy couscous

2 tbsp coleslaw

1/2 red pepper, chopped

Handful of spicy green olives, chopped

Boiled egg, sliced

One gherkin, chopped

One thick slice of cheddar cheese, chopped into bite-size pieces

A few turkey slices

Handful of rocket (place this in the centre of the plate and a glug of olive oil over)

One tsp Dijon mustard/mayo/chutney

Toasted pitta bread, to serve

After everything is cut up, place all the ingredients on a plate — you decide how you want to eat. Mairéad is a mix-it-all-up person and I am an individual picker.

The weekly shop

M I won't try and compete with Jenny's fabulous recipes but my top tip for coping with the endless question of what's for dinner is to make a meal plan, then a shopping list to match it. If you are still like Jenny and find yourself wandering around a supermarket three times a week, please stop, and try online shopping (more on this later)!

When I was a child, every Friday my mother collected me from school in Finglas West and we would go to do the big weekly food shop. I always loved this time because it signalled the start of the weekend. We would have chats, *and* I got a Choc Dip.

The Friday ritual involved going to three different places: Crazy Prices in Janelle Shopping centre, Gus — the fruit and veg shop — and finally, Dolan's butchers.

I've often wondered what weird time zone my mam lived in, because she seemed to get so much more done than I can do now. Her daily cooking and baking looked hassle-free and I never, ever heard her say, 'I don't know what to do for dinner tonight' ... ever.

But although we are inundated with more convenience foods now, today's families always seem so stretched when it comes to time. Maybe it's all the after-school activities or the organised play-dates or the commutes or the scrolling, but there is no way in any given week that I would have an entire afternoon to dedicate to the big food shop.

I've gotten better at managing my time, but that involves saying 'no' to lots of things in order to get the essentials done. About three years ago, I started to say no to physically going to the supermarket unless I absolutely had to. At first I was reluctant, but I am now a gold medallist superfast champion of online food shopping and with the vouchers available, delivery is generally free!*

Why waste your time finding a trolley token then going all around the supermarket, picking up the spuds and carrots, squeezing the sliced pan to make sure it's fresh, looking for the chicken, the pasta, the butter, the rice, the 40 apples, the three litres of milk, the eggs on top so they don't get damaged, the extra heavy bottle of detergent, then putting it all on the conveyor belt, the beeps, then packing and finally lugging the eight bags for life into the boot of the car … when there is a brilliant service that will do it all for you?

There has been the odd error – a lost item or an extra that I didn't order – but that's also happened when I've gone to the shops myself.

And it works for everyone. Busy parents of newborns, you can do a shop at 3 a.m.; workers who are gone all day, you can arrange for it to arrive at 7 p.m. or on a Saturday morning; and it's life-changing for people who don't drive.

*Getting your shopping delivered costs about €8, but I always have a voucher for a tenner so the entire service costs me *nada*. If you are not taking advantage of your shopping vouchers, who are you? Every supermarket has their own voucher scheme and ultimately if you shop regularly you will get the best value.

Get someone else to do this

What we know now about →

movies & books

OR, WHY *WHEN HARRY MET SALLY* IS THE BEST MOVIE OF ALL TIME

I t's a running joke in most friends' WhatsApp groups that getting everyone to agree on a date to meet up is an impossible task. So the idea of getting your girl gang up and out to the cinema may seem like a wild fantasy, but, wait a second ... what about a friends' watch party? These were big during lockdown, when it was literally impossible to meet up, and streaming services like Netflix and Amazon Prime all got in on the act. It's a way of syncing your movie of choice with all your mates so that you can watch together in real time (while texting or commenting online). So get the popcorn out — or whatever you're having yourself — and let's talk movies.

Sticky floors and smuggled sweets

M My first cinema memory is going with my much older sister Simone and her then–boyfriend to see *Santa Claus: The Movie* in the Savoy cinema in Dublin. The comfortable plush red velvet seats, the gigantic screen and, to top it off, a Christmas film!

But life changed in the early '90s in Finglas when we got our own two-screen cinema beside Janelle Shopping Centre. It was right across the road from my home. It was affectionately known as Sticky Floors because ... well, it had very sticky floors. For a time, they had a strictly enforced rule that only food purchased on the premises could be eaten there. We had so much craic smuggling in our sweets from home. Only once was I caught, and they made me hand over my two Kimberly biscuits and packet of crisps, but they returned them after *Jurassic Park*.

Cinema dates

When dates kicked in for me, the cinema was always the perfect place to go because it meant I could be with the person that I really fancied without the added pressure of talking to him, too. All of my energy had been used up getting my winged eyeliner straight. (Although this meant I went to see *Titanic* three times with three different boys … my heart did indeed go on.)

Now, having spent the last 16 or so years only going to the cinema to see kids' films (I think I have seen every single one), I love seeing a movie of my choice on my time. Some of the greats are over three hours long and I just cannot commit to that in one sitting, so I really enjoy splitting them over two nights (like any normal person).

Film is real, genuine escapism, where you can be transported to a different country, different century or even a different world altogether for a few hours, and with popcorn it is pure bliss.

My taste in films is comedies, rom-coms, true stories … anything heartwarming, uplifting and tear-jerking. I'm OK with mild violence, but anything beyond that is a hard no. I don't care if it's up for ten Oscars — there's enough of that in the real world, so I personally can't allow it into my entertainment time too (but then I love a true crime podcast, so go figure?).

The horror!

J There was no such thing as too much TV or too many movies in my house when I was growing up. We LOVED IT. Myself and my sister were big horror fans, and we watched it all: *Hammer House of Horror, Friday the 13th, Nightmare on Elm Street, Scanners, The Shining, The Exorcist, The Fly, Pet Sematary* ... I showed *The Evil Dead* to a group of traumatised classmates at a sleepover on my twelfth birthday. Whenever I meet up with one of them, they still talk about this. The crazy thing is that I cannot watch horror movies now. I think it's since I had my own children: horror is too much for me now (and the same goes for Stephen King's novels — I read him for years but can't anymore).

I remember long summers walking down to the video shop and renting out three or four movies to keep us going. And it wasn't just horror; I watched all the old black-and-whites and classics that were shown on TV, too — like *Gone With the Wind, Casablanca, Singing in the Rain, The Birds, High Society, Bringing up Baby, Lawrence of Arabia, All About Eve* and *Some Like It Hot*.

So, to choose a favourite movie for me is almost impossible, but if I had to, I'd say ... *E.T.* It evokes so many gorgeous memories for me and is a brilliant movie to boot. I've watched it so many times I've lost count and will continue to watch it for years to come.

There are movie lists out there for everything, but if I had to make up a list of movies to watch with your best friends, here are the ones I'd include.

Jenny's movie list

Romcoms

- **Something's Gotta Give** – Jack Nicholson and Diane Keaton in a Nancy Meyers romantic comedy. I love this movie. It's so funny and lovely to see older people navigating love – nothing ever really changes!

- **Amélie** – It's French, it's beautiful and it will bring you joy.

- **Four Weddings and a Funeral** – Where we really got to meet Hugh Grant for the first time. Perfect!

- **Bridget Jones's Diary** – The book brought to life by the brilliant Renée Zellweger.

- **Jerry Maguire** – Love any movie with Tom Cruise, but this is up there with his best ones.

- **Ferris Bueller's Day Off** – Mathew Broderick will always be Ferris to me.

Comedies

- **Meet The Parents** – Ben Stiller and Robert De Niro … milking cat nipples.

- **There's Something about Mary** – I'll never forget the zip scene!

- **Some Like it Hot** – A classic starring Marilyn Monroe, Tony Curtis and Jack Lemmon – so funny and quick.

- **Zoolander** – Ben Stiller and Owen Wilson are 'really, really good looking' – and hilarious.

- **Bridesmaids** – A brilliant, laugh-out-loud script and an amazing female cast.

Movies to cry at

- **Life is Beautiful** – Italian drama about hope and humour always winning out.

- **Titanic** – The love story of Jack and Rose – and the true story of the *Titanic* brought to life.

- **Little Miss Sunshine** – A family road trip with a difference.

- **Up** – The opener to this animated Disney classic still gets me every time.

- **Steel Magnolias** – Starring Sally Field, Dolly Parton, Shirley MacLaine and Daryl Hannah, and featuring female friendships and loss ... and crying, lots of crying!

- **Beaches** – An oldie but a goodie starring Bette Midler and Barbara Hershey – a real tear-jerker.

- **Cinema Paradiso** – One of my favourite movies, about the life-affirming relationship between a young Sicilian boy and a movie projectionist.

- **Past Lives** – Tells the story of classmates Nora and Hae Sung as they grow up, and all the 'what if's of life. Gorgeous.

Mairéad's movie list

When Harry Met Sally This is my favourite film of all time. I never tire of watching it. Meg Ryan and Billy Crystal's chemistry, New York City in all its glory, the most beautiful soundtrack and that perpetual question — can men and women ever just be friends?

La La Land Set in LA, where everyone is trying to make their dreams come true, this is a colourful love story about how a decision made today can change the outcome of all your tomorrows. The musical theme for characters Mia (Emma Stone) and Sebastian (Ryan Gosling) is a beautiful piece that's sprinkled throughout the film.

Muriel's Wedding Toni Collette is perfection in this film. This ticks all the boxes for me — it's hilarious, it's desperately sad and it's full of ABBA songs.

Gone with the Wind Viven Leigh is iconic as Scarlett O'Hara in this classic. Made in the 1930s and set during the American Civil War, it's an epic love story, but also a story about the love we feel for home. All her life, Scarlett believes she is in love with Ashley, but he loves his wife, Melanie. And when it's too late, Scarlett realises that she actually loves her own husband, Rhett, but by then he's had enough and leaves her with the famous line, 'Frankly, my dear, I don't give a damn.' *Gone with the Wind* is also where I got my daughter Bonnie's name from (Scarlett and Rhett had one child called Bonnie Blue Butler).

The joy of a good book

J Is there anything nicer than walking into a book shop? Everything about it sings to me. I have a fantasy of owning my own book shop so I could spend my days wandering around touching, smelling and reading books. I love that feeling of excitement when a book calls to you and you take it down from the shelf, open that first page and begin to read. That feeling of being sucked into the author's world and blocking out the reality of life. I think maybe that's why I love reading so much; being able to live others' lives through the pages of a book, to travel to far-flung lands and live out exciting dramas and experiences. A good book allows all of this while not having to leave your very warm, cosy couch.

I love reading because it is solitary and silent. Once I am in the book, I am gone from this world. People can be talking around me or to me and I am oblivious. I've been this way since I was a child. Books have been a constant in my life and my bedside table spills over with books. Yes, I am one of those terrible people who reads multiple books at the same time. It's like a little lottery when I get into bed … what do I feel like tonight? Of course, there are those very special books that don't allow for this. They consume you and won't get out of your head. You are unable to think of anything else but the characters and story in the book. That is magic. I would choose books over everything else — music, films, TV … if I didn't have books, my life would be duller and greyer.

I think the books that we read and love when we are children and young adults can have a massive effect on our reading for the rest of our lives. That's why some of my favourite books are from my youth. They ignited something inside me that has burnt bright for all these years.

- *Pet Sematary* by Stephen King
- The *Adrian Mole* series by Sue Townsend
- *Are You There, God? It's Me, Margaret* by Judy Blume
- *The Little Prince* by Antoine de Saint-Exupéry
- *A Prayer for Owen Meany* by John Irving

6

You can find find magic wherever you look.

Sit back and relax, all you need is a *book.* ,

DR SEUSS

The gift that kept on giving

M In April 2020, a month into the pandemic, I celebrated my 40th birthday. We couldn't travel beyond 2km from our home, so it meant that the only loved ones (besides Louis and the kids) I saw were on Zoom. So, Jenny came up with a genius gift idea. She posted a book to me every month for the entire year, each with a handwritten note inside explaining why she'd chosen it for me. It was so thoughtful and perfect, because just as I would finish one, the postman would arrive with the next. During much of that time, we couldn't physically see each other, so it was like getting a hug in the post from Jenny. And, proving how well she knows me, I LOVED 11 out of the 12. That's an excellent strike rate. That gift gave me so much more than 12 books; it forced me to carve out time for reading books again (and not just newspapers). Now I can have three books on the go at one time.

My favourites from my year of books were:

- **Where'd you go, Bernadette** by Maria Semple
- **The Dutch House** by Ann Patchett
- **The Little Prince** by Antoine de Saint-Exupéry
- **French Braid** by Anne Tyler
- **I Feel Bad About My Neck** by Nora Ephron

This is one of the most beautiful books you will ever read! **J**

I LOVE READING BECAUSE IT IS SOLITARY AND SILENT. ONCE I AM IN THE BOOK, I AM GONE FROM THIS WORLD.

What we know now about →

what matters

OR, WHY BUSYNESS IS NOT A BADGE OF HONOUR

This is your one precious life

J We waste so much of our life filling up our days with a lot of not very important things. One of my favourite poems is Mary Oliver's 'The Summer Day'. Even if you don't know the poem, you will have heard the line 'Tell me, what is it you plan to do with your one wild and precious life?' The funny thing about only reading this line is that it could sound like a call to panic in a kind of 'Aaaggghhh, I'm running out of time, I need to do stuff nowww' way, when in fact the poem is about the exact opposite. It's about taking time out 'to be idle [...] to stroll through the fields', to stop rushing and to take time to notice all the beauty surrounding you. This is hard to do if you are always working off a SHIT–TO–DO LIST, but here's the thing – that list WILL NEVER END. You are going to keep adding to that list for ever unless you stop. Imagine that.

I'm not talking about packing a bag and legging it from your responsibilities (one can dream), we all have to do the feckin' food shop and clean our homes, work, pick up children and bring them to activities, look after elderly parents, etc. BUT these are just life things, I'm talking about the other things you tell yourself you HAVE TO DO. Guess what? You don't.

- You don't have to visit three friends a week
- You don't have to attend every PTA meeting
- You don't have to go for work drinks
- You don't have to answer every phone call
- You don't have to have coffee with that person you don't really want to go for coffee with!

These are choices you are making under obligation to others so that you don't let anyone down or upset them. It is not your job to make others happy. *It is your job to make sure you are happy.* No one and nothing can make you happy except you. Mic drop. And I guarantee you if you start prioritising your time for you, you will become happier. You will feel less stressed, less put upon, less anxious and less irritated. We women have to just stop.

Busyness is not a badge of honour

I know someone who is always in a rush, puffing and panting and making lists and running out the door to get somewhere or pick someone up. Complaining about having to call someone or having to do the shop and what will they have for dinner tonight and where do all the hours in the day go. It's all a bit much to be around. I feel stressed in her company because she is always talking about the things she has to do or has failed to do or will have to do another day. Does she do this because she thinks it's busyness that makes her important? That having no time makes her needed and somewhat superior to others who have nothing in the diary that day? Compare this with a friend of mine who is the most laid-back person I know. Time doesn't seem to impinge on her life. She floats around without a mobile phone, swimming in the sea, drinking coffee, carefree and unhurried. That doesn't mean she doesn't get things done — she does, but in an intentional way without any flapping. I envy this lack of flapping.

Can I make a suggestion? Before you go adding something else into the diary, ask yourself, is it really necessary? Is it something you actually want to do, or something you feel obliged to do? Try leaving the diary page blank and see what happens. I guarantee you won't regret it!

Are you your own time-thief?

M Well, Jenny has pointed out to me that my toxic trait was filling my time (I use the past tense because I've improved greatly) but growing up, I don't ever remember anyone really relaxing at home, apart from on Sundays when all the shops were closed and we ate a roast dinner. But the clean-up after felt like the juice wasn't worth the squeeze. Then both my parents would fall asleep because I'm sure they were both shattered from the week that had gone by. But relaxing or being idle in my home in Finglas was seen as a sin and I think that's the same for many Irish women of a certain era — must be the Catholic guilt or something.

Simple maths (or 'Is this worth my time?')

I was never great at maths in secondary school and did ordinary level for my Leaving Cert. In fact, maths scared me a little. I told my teacher, Ms Stokes, who said, 'Make maths your friend, Mairéad!'

So I did, and now I use maths almost every day. But I mainly use it to measure my time. When I get asked to do anything, from job offers to joining a committee, I use maths to see if I can do the 'ask' or should I say 'no', because we can't help ourselves. We (women) are people-pleasers. We are all guilty of saying, 'Yeah, sure, I'd love to', and regretting it later.

Do the maths on your time before saying yes to the stress.

Mairéad introduced me to her simple maths idea, which I think is genius in its simplicity. It will really get you to think before accepting a job or an evening out.

Example: you've been asked to join the local sports committee. It's just once a week on Tuesday nights for roughly an hour ... and you're free on Tuesday nights. They meet at 7.30 p.m. each week. Let's do the maths.

- You arrive home at 6.30 p.m. from work on Tuesdays.
- Dinner will have to be inhaled by 7 p.m.
- You will leave the house at 7.15 p.m. to get there on time.
- Meeting won't start until 7.40 p.m. and will finish at 8.45 p.m.
- You'll get home at 9 p.m. when it's time for bed.
- Wednesday night is the kids' swimming lessons, so that looks the same for you.
- Thursday evening, you call in to your elderly mother after work.

It's NOT just Tuesday night. It's the lack of downtime on that day and what happens in the days before and after too.

I'm not telling you to shy away from volunteering or taking part in local committees or clubs because I know you get so much back, too. What I am saying is, *don't be volunTOLD to do it*.

Take back your time and use it to create a life you dreamt of living.

Shit To-Do lists
and Nice To-Do lists

I We were talking on the podcast about the fact that the to-do list is NEVER-ENDING. Just when you feel all chuffed with yourself drawing lines through what you've done, you have to add more things to it — IT NEVER ENDS. Some of the things on the Shit To-Do List include: food shopping, making dinner, cleaning the house, buying toilet rolls, clothes washing, paying bills, getting the car serviced ... and on and on and on.

So, we had an idea — what about making up a Nice To-Do List? This is a list of things that you would like to do, places to go, future goals and dreams. Some of them you may do one day, others are distant dreams that, just maybe, you might do in this lifetime. Here are some of mine:

- Go to Japan (Ray said to me 'It's a long way to go to be disappointed.' He is, of course, wrong. It will be AMAZING.)
- Take up horseriding again
- Go to Crufts
- Write more books
- Adopt a donkey
- Visit Bhutan
- Take some courses in counselling and psychotherapy
- Go to Wimbledon
- Take some conversational French classes
- Go hiking in Germany and stay in one of those mountain huts

- Travel to European destinations doing half-marathons with Mairéad (what better way to see a city than with a gentle jog while looking at all the sights?)
- Try acting again
- Do a 10-day silent meditation retreat ... Mairéad said she'd only manage one day, so maybe start with that first

It's fun, isn't it? When you give yourself the freedom to sit and write down some of the things you'd actually like to do, initially you might be a bit stuck. Stay with it. Give yourself time. And then once you start, you will see that list grow. Keep coming back to it and adding to it. You will see that there are so many things you would like to do and achieve. It's a lovely list that you can come back to again and again with no pressure. And things that you did want to do might change and you can delete them and add a new thing in. Then take one thing on the list and take your first step towards achieving it.

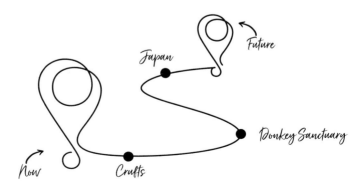

To-do or not-to-do list

(M) Back when I was a student, I worked in a busy Dubin nightclub. The boss there wrote a list of jobs you had to do and put them in order of priority. So when I arrived in to the office I would go to his desk, look for the A4 page with my name written on the top, take it and get cracking. He did this for all employees.

At the end of the shift, I would hand back the list with a line through the jobs that had been completed. It was this that made me fall in love with lists and I took immense satisfaction in crossing off what I had done. But now that I'm an actual adult and in charge of younger humans, the to-do list is not a list anymore. It's a to-do conveyor belt that is never-ending. As soon as one thing is crossed off, five more things are added.

IT. IS. EXHAUSTING.

So, Jenny and I talked about creating the Nice To-Do List. One that will probably never get done in its entirety and that can contain things that are most likely never going to happen. But we can add to it and, every now and then, do something on it and cross it off – DONE. (Tick!) Here's my current Nice To-Do List:

- Learn yoga – properly
- Go to the Eurovision again
- Eat chocolate with Roger Federer
- Watch *Gone With the Wind* start to finish without interruption (probably more chance of chocolate with Roger than this)

- Continue to play piano

- Write that book

- Take a long cooking course

- Get a second dog ← *Are you SURE about this, Mairéad?* 🅙

- Print off those family photos

- Vist Dunmore East alone three times a year

- Run a marathon (an odd Nice To-Do thing, but I really want to do it)

- Do a one-day silent retreat with Jenny (this will be tricky, but we love a challenge)

- Go back to education – but don't take exams (I want to sit in lecture halls, listen and learn, but have no interest in the examination part)

- Visit Japan with Jenny to see the cherry blossoms (we will NOT be disappointed, Ray)

- Plant my potted hydrangea into soil

- Drink tea by the sea with Jennyyyyyy

Inspired? We've left the next page blank for you to start your very own Nice To–Do List.

Odd, but I really want to do it:
run a marathon

My nice To-Do List

Get writing

When life gives you lemons
– make a vision board

I had spent years asking (a.k.a. praying to) the Lord Jesus and Mary (never Joseph because I've been let down by too many carpenters) for things. But now I don't have to pray anymore. All I had to do was ask the universe ... and while I was at it, create a vision board.

What's a vision board?

It's exactly what it says on the tin (or in this case, the board). It's filled with images, photos or affirmations that represent the changes you'd like to see happen in your life. They could be around career ambitions, personal relationship desires or lifestyle goals. Even Oprah has admitted to using them in the past.

Dr. Frank Niles, a social scientist, says, 'When we visualise an act, the brain generates an impulse that tells our neurons to "perform" the movement – meaning the act of visualising the goal can be nearly as powerful as the experience.' Obviously the asks need to be somewhat realistic. You can't put down a photoshopped image of you winning Wimbledon if you're 40 and don't play tennis.

The vision board needs to sit in a place where you will see it often and you must focus on it daily and visualise yourself in the scenario pinned to your board.

So now I confess to almighty God, and to you, my brothers and sisters, that once upon a time I created my own vision board.

On a Saturday night in 2009 when it felt like everyone else in my world was out having a great time, I sat down with a large piece of cardboard, the good scissors and a fresh Pritt Stick. I cut out images from magazines and some affirmations I had printed off (embarrassingly, during a lunch break in Today FM). It all felt like a very teenagery thing to do, but here I was, a grown woman with a sleeping child upstairs. This was done during a particularly low point in my life which coincided with the very high sales of *The Secret*, the first book that sold manifesting to the (female) masses.

Manifesting sounds easy ... almost *too* easy.

- Ask the universe
- Believe
- Then receive

I thought the idea of it was horse manure, but after creating what looked like a third-class school project (my vision board), I soon noticed a change in me and how I behaved. The board and manifesting was all about calmness, which was missing in every area of my life, work, home, family and friends.

My vision board

Life Firstly, I glued a photo of a lit candle with a pretty glow. To me this seemed like a good place to start because with my Catholic upbringing I lit hundreds of candles over the years, and all of them had a special intention or a prayer attached to them.

Relationship An image of a couple holding hands. At the time I saw this as a symbol of closeness, togetherness and connection.

Family A photo of a mother and son just being together. I desperately wanted more downtime with Dara, who was a toddler at the time.

Career While my career was in a good spot, I was really disorganised and everything I did (even if I did it well) was very last-minute. So I used an image of an organised work desk, a pen placed just where you need it, a phone, a vase with flowers – everything was clean, fresh, serene and sorted.

Pet At this point in my life I had never owned a pet, but knew I had always wanted one. In a way this seemed like the easiest goal to manifest, but I didn't have the hours or funds to have a dog at that time. So, a cute picture on my vision board was as good as it would get.

I also wrote a list stating what each picture represented. While there are no instructions for manifesting, the guidelines say to write a list of roughly ten things you would like to see happen or change in your life. The language you use must be positive and present tense. You then arrange them in order of importance.

The outcome?

Spoiler alert — IT WORKED! There is no science to back this up, but I firmly believe that seeing what I wanted to change in my life laid out in front of me every day focused my mind. In a matter of weeks, I could see things changing.

My life became less hectic because I was more organised at work. That led me to have more free time after work to just be with Dara. A relationship did come along when I least expected it, and the pet (Murphy) arrived eventually. The strange thing with a manifesting list is that there is usually a thread between all the wanted goals; one feeds another.

Take two ... Dancing with the Stars

The next time I thought, 'OK, right, let's really give this manifesting a go again,' was when I took part in season three of *Dancing with the Stars*. In the early days of training I was still breastfeeding Bonnie and I had less than zero fitness. Then the bookies released their predictions. I was 33 to 1 to win (second from the bottom). Not a chance. I'd be gone by week three.

But each week I visualised finishing my dance with no errors and then hearing our names get called to go through to the following week. The weeks rolled on. I was still there. Eat, rinse tan, dance rehearsals and repeat. I always visualised getting to the final – sure, what was the point in manifesting if I didn't?

In all those visualisations, I saw myself wearing a gold dress at the final – so I was really excited to see my show dance dress. I tried to hide my disappointment when I saw it for the first time because it was a greeny-blue colour, and then I was told, 'It's teal.' Teal is very far from gold. The day before the final, the creative director watched John and I rehearse. He called us over and said, shaking his head, 'That costume isn't working on you, Mairéad, I'm going to have to find something else.' He eventually came back to me with a bright yellow dress that was covered in tiny gold stones. Bingo! My manifesting was working overtime.

Part of my manifesting was that, each night before I went to sleep, I imagined Jennifer Zamparelli saying, 'The winners of *Dancing with the Stars* 2019 are ...' *be–le dum dum dum dum, be–le dum dum dum dum, be– le dum dum dum dum* (tension music) '... Mairéad and John!'

And that's exactly what happened. I didn't mortify myself too much, I stayed until the very end, I wore a gold(ish) dress ... and I won.

Maybe it was the hours and hours of rehearsals.

Maybe it's because I was given the best dance pro partner in John Nolan.

Maybe it's because I was lucky with song choices and dances.

OR maybe it was down to my universal manifesting?

I've not yet used this a third time. I feel a little bit like Aladdin – this next wish might be my last – so I'm saving it for an emergency manifest.

THE ACT OF
VISUALISING
THE GOAL
CAN BE
NEARLY AS
POWERFUL
AS THE
EXPERIENCE.

Managing expectations

J When I was writing about being human, I wrote that it seems to be the human condition to constantly chase happiness and run from anything unhappy or difficult. Buddhism would say that this is what causes suffering and why we as humans are never satisfied. How to overcome this dissatisfaction? By getting real about the fact that life is just a series of events unfolding in front of you. Different moments that will come and go. By not grasping and desperately trying to cling on to the good things (happiness) or run screaming from the bad things (unhappiness) our lives become so much more even keeled and calm. Nothing remains the same. Everything is constantly changing. Our situations, our moods, our families, our friends, how our coffee tastes ... everything! By really allowing this truth to seep into our reality we allow our lives to transform and become more peaceful and balanced. It's all about managing our life expectations.

Manifesting or woo-woo

Let's get this straight. There is no scientific basis to manifesting. You can believe something and it can still not be true ... but I am a big believer in the power of positive thinking. Again, absolutely no science to back this up, but I think it makes life a hell of a lot easier. I am a glass-half-full person, and I am glad to be. Negativity is sometimes dressed up as realism and practicality, but it can be draining to be around and sucks the joy out of life. I like to think positively, and I think it has made my life easier because:

- I believe that most things will work out.

- I believe that people are generally good and kind.

● I believe if I work hard and give something my all that it will be successful (how I measure success is a different story).

And so, as woo-woo as manifesting sounds, I think there is something in it. It forces a focus, a positive projection of wants, a dream to follow through on. It is not about conjuring up winning the lotto and then crying for a week when it doesn't happen. It is more about putting out positive vibes and seeing what comes back at you. So, for example, say you are single and looking to meet someone. You are not looking for that person to complete you, you are just open to meeting someone to share your time with. If you put this in the zone of manifesting, maybe you write down the type of person you would like to meet (as you have read, Mairéad knows all about this). You have now put this out into the universe. You are announcing to yourself and your general vibeness that you are open to meeting someone. I am positive that this changes your overall demeanour. How you hold yourself, how you interact with others – you have positive vibes shooting out of you in all directions. People are more likely to respond to you in a positive way or at least view you in a positive light. The minor irritations of life become a bit less of a big deal, you stop taking things and yourself so seriously and are just open to possibilities, maybe saying 'yes' a little bit more. All of these ways of being are, in a sense, manifesting. You are making a conscious decision to put your best foot forward and this can only have a positive return. The same goes for a job or friendship – by putting out your intentions, you are lighting up the way for manifesting your wants and dreams. And anyway, like I said, there is no scientific basis to this at all, so what have you got to lose?

Now,
time to say goodbye

This is the hard bit. To try and wrap this all up in a perfect neat bow so that we can close the book together and breathe a sigh of relief with the knowledge that we are all sorted now.

Sorry! That's not going to happen. If we've learned anything by writing this book it's that there is no such thing as perfect – and we don't like bows, anyway. Over the years we have both realised that there is no one way of doing anything. You have to find what works for you, and that usually means making a lot of mistakes along the way. But maybe, with the help of this book, you can see that those so-called mistakes are what make us the messy, wonderful, muddled-up people that we are. The truth is that we are all a little bit fragile and that is what makes us human.

But like we said in the beginning of the book, we all need constant reminders to live in the NOW – and we think we should end how we started, with a list of things to try to remember on a daily basis.

1.

You will be dead forever – remember this and repeat it often.

This will hopefully allow you to stop worrying and stressing about stupid shit and focus your attention on what matters right NOW.

2.

Find out what brings you joy and try to do a lot of it.

It could be as simple as walking in nature, swimming in the sea, spending time with your loved ones, your career. Only you know what this is, but when you find out, give it your focus, time and energy.

3.

How you look is the least interesting thing about you.

We all have insecurities about how we look. Recognise this in yourself and others. Wear the shorts, put on the togs, buy the sleeveless top. We are all perfectly imperfect, and that's what makes us human.

4.

This too shall pass – the good and the bad.

If you are having a great day, appreciate it but know it will pass. If you are having a shit day, understand that it too shall pass. It's a cliché but tomorrow is another day. There is always hope.

5.

Surround yourself with people who make you feel good about yourself.

Do not put up with bad behaviour. Life is too short to hang out with assholes.

6.

Be kind to yourself.

Listen more and be patient with yourself.

7.

Every experience is a life lesson.

Mark it down, learn from it and move on.

8.

You can't have it all.

Nor should you attempt to have it all. It will always end in disaster.
Take your time in making a big decision, quieten down, block out all
external noise and listen to yourself. You know what is best for you.
Trust yourself.

9.

It is not your job to make others happy.

It is your job to make sure you are happy, and the rest will follow.

10.

And we have to end on ten, so …

get an air fryer, get out in nature, buy a spray mop, invest in a good
hairdryer and leave your lips alone.

NOW,
WE HOPE
YOU KNOW ...
YOU ARE
ENOUGH.

LOVE,
JENNY AND
MAIRÉAD xx

Acknowledgements

THANK YOU to my husband, Ray, and children,
Kate and Tom, for all your love, support and encouragement.
I do think I deserve a 'she shed' after all this?

A gigantic thank you to my husband, Louis,
my almost–adult, Dara, and my girls, Eliza and Bonnie —
I love you lot too much.

We think everyone knows this already, but just in case you didn't, it takes a whole team of people to put a book together. These are the people that we could not have done it without:

First and foremost, Teresa Daly, our editor, therapist and friend. You made us both believe we could do this from day one. Your calming influence and hand–holding got us over the finish line and we are both so grateful to you. Let's do it again sometime!

To Aoibheann Molumby and all the editorial team. You took our pages and worked your magic. We felt put together after all your help (like a good haircut or good bra). Thank you for your wonderful support.

To Mia O'Reilly, the calmest and coolest publicist we know. Thank you for all the chats and for organising us in such a delightful way.

To everyone behind the scenes in Gill. We may not have met you directly, but we thank you! The people who work in a company make the company — and Gill Books' happy atmosphere is testament to that.

A book like ours is all about the life lessons that have got us this far and so to life we say a huge, big THANK YOU! Even during the shitty times when we both may have cursed you, the truth is that those crappy times have made us who we are today — and for that we are grateful.

To our podcast listeners — you were the inspiration behind this whole book! We wanted our book to be like the podcast on paper. We wanted it to read like how we talk on the podcast and how we react to things that you tell us. Thank you for listening along, telling us your thoughts and giving us huge laughs. And thank you for buying our book.

And to end on a high, remember, everyone: 'You'll be dead forever.'